Hands-On Python and Practical Data Science with Python

Preface

Who This Book Is For
"Hands-On Python and Pandas" is for aspiring data scientists and Python users eager to master data analysis with Pandas. Whether you're a beginner or have some experience, this book will help you apply Python and Pandas to real-world data problems.

How This Book Is Organized
The book is divided into eight parts:

1. **Introduction to Python and Pandas**

2. **Essential Operations**

3. **Data Cleaning and Transformation**

4. **Data Analysis with Pandas**

5. **Visualization with Pandas**

6. **Performance and Optimization**

7. **Real-World Applications**

8. **Projects**
   Each chapter builds on the previous one with practical, hands-on code examples.

What Was Left Out
This book doesn't cover the basics of Python programming or advanced topics like machine learning, focusing instead on intermediate-level data manipulation and analysis using Pandas.

Code Style (About the Code)
The code follows Python's PEP 8 style guide for consistency and readability, with detailed explanations to help you understand each step.

Release Notes
The first edition includes the latest techniques and best practices for using

Pandas. Future updates will be documented in release notes.

Notes on the First Edition

This edition covers core concepts and practical applications, with step-by-step examples to make learning easy and accessible.

MechatronicsLAB Online Learning

Visit mechatronicslab.net for more resources.
Contact: mechatronicslab@gmail.com

Acknowledgments for the First Edition

Thanks to the MechatronicsLAB team and my family for their support during the creation of this book.

Copyright

Disclaimer

Table of Content

Chapter-1 Introduction to Python and Pandas

What is Python?

Python is a high-level, general-purpose programming language that emphasizes readability and simplicity. Created by Guido van Rossum and first released in 1991, Python is known for its clean syntax, ease of learning, and versatility. It supports multiple programming paradigms, including procedural, object-oriented, and functional programming.

Key Features of Python:

1. **Simple Syntax**: Python's syntax is straightforward and resembles natural language, making it easy to learn and use.
2. **Interpreted Language**: Python code is executed line by line, which allows for quick prototyping and testing.
3. **Extensive Standard Library**: Python comes with a comprehensive standard library that simplifies tasks like file handling, web development, and data analysis.
4. **Cross-Platform**: Python programs can run on various operating systems, including Windows, macOS, and Linux.
5. **Active Community**: A large, active community provides support, tutorials, and third-party libraries for Python development.

Introduction to Pandas

Pandas is an open-source Python library used for data manipulation and analysis. Built on top of NumPy, it provides high-performance, easy-to-use data structures and tools for working with structured data.

Key Features of Pandas:

1. **Data Structures**:
   a. **Series**: A one-dimensional array-like structure with labeled indices.
   b. **DataFrame**: A two-dimensional, tabular data structure with labeled rows and columns.
2. **Data Manipulation**: Tools to reshape, merge, and filter datasets.
3. **Missing Data Handling**: Functions to identify, clean, and fill missing data.
4. **Data Analysis**: Built-in methods for aggregation, grouping, and

descriptive statistics.

5. **File Handling**: Seamlessly read from and write to various file formats, such as CSV, Excel, and SQL.

Installation

Installing Python and Pandas on Different Platforms

Windows:

1. Download the latest Python installer from the official Python website.
2. Run the installer and ensure the option "Add Python to PATH" is checked.
3. After installation, open Command Prompt and verify Python is installed by typing: `python --version`
4. Install Pandas using pip: `pip install pandas`

macOS:

1. macOS often comes with Python pre-installed. To check, open Terminal and type: `python3 --version`

2. If Python is not installed, download it from the official Python website or use Homebrew: `brew install python`

3. Install Pandas using pip: `pip3 install pandas`

Linux:

1. Most Linux distributions include Python. Verify the installation by typing: `python3 --version`
2. If Python is not installed, use the package manager of your distribution. For example, on Ubuntu: `sudo apt update`
   `sudo apt install python3`
   `sudo apt install python3-pip`
3. Install Pandas using pip: `pip3 install pandas`

Verification Steps for Installation

After installing Python and Pandas, verify the installations:

1. Open your terminal or command prompt.
2. Verify Python installation by typing: `python --version   # or python3 --version on macOS/Linux`
3. Verify Pandas installation by opening a Python shell and typing: `import pandas as pd`

```
print(pd.__version__)
```
If no errors occur and a version number is printed, the installation was successful.

MacOS and Linux Specificity

- If permission errors occur when using `pip`, use the `--user` flag:
  ```
  pip install pandas --user
  ```
- On Linux, some distributions require additional dependencies for Python. Install them using the package manager (e.g., `sudo apt install python3-dev` on Ubuntu).

Alternative Installation Methods For an easier setup or for managing multiple Python environments, consider using Anaconda:

1. Download and install Anaconda from the official website.
2. Create a new environment: `conda create -n myenv python=3.9 pandas`

3. Activate the environment: `conda activate myenv`

4. Test the setup: `import pandas as pd`
   ```
   print(pd.__version__)
   ```

Sample Code Testing After installation, test Pandas with the following sample code:

```
import pandas as pd
# Creating a simple DataFrame
data = {
    "Name": ["Alice", "Bob", "Charlie"],
    "Age": [25, 30, 35],
    "City": ["New York", "Los Angeles", "Chicago"]
}
df = pd.DataFrame(data)
print(df)


# Display basic information
print("\nBasic Info:")
print(df.info())
```

This will print the DataFrame and some basic information, confirming that Pandas is installed and working correctly.

Chapter-2 Basics of Python Programming for Pandas

Before diving into Pandas, a solid understanding of Python programming basics is essential. This chapter covers the foundational Python concepts required to use Pandas effectively, including working with data structures, loops, functions, and libraries.

Key Characteristics of Python Basics for Pandas:
- **Data Types:** Covers fundamental data types like integers, floats, strings, and Booleans.
- **Data Structures:** Explains lists, dictionaries, tuples, and sets, which are integral to data manipulation.
- **Loops and Conditionals:** Provides a framework for iterating and conditional operations.
- **Functions:** Demonstrates how to write reusable code blocks.
- **Library Integration:** Highlights Python's ecosystem for importing and utilizing external libraries.

Basic Rules for Python Programming:
1. Understand Python syntax and indentation.
2. Know how to declare and manipulate variables and data structures.
3. Write functions to perform repetitive tasks.
4. Utilize loops and conditionals to process data efficiently.
5. Import and use external libraries effectively.

Best Practices:
- **Write Readable Code:** Use meaningful variable and function names.
- **Comment Your Code:** Document logic for better understanding and maintenance.
- **Follow Pythonic Principles:** Emphasize simplicity and readability.
- **Leverage Built-In Functions:** Use Python's extensive standard library.
- **Practice Regularly:** Reinforce concepts through exercises and projects.

Syntax Table:

SL No	Concept	Syntax/Example	Description
1	Declare Variables	`x = 5`	Assigns a value to a variable.
2	Use Lists	`my_list = [1, 2, 3]`	Creates a list to store multiple items.
3	Write a Function	`def my_function():`	Defines a reusable block of code.
4	Loop Through Data	`for item in my_list:`	Iterates over elements in a list.
5	Import Libraries	`import pandas as pd`	Imports an external library.

Syntax Explanation:

1. Declare Variables

What is Declare Variables?

Assigns a value to a variable, allowing it to store data that can be accessed and manipulated throughout the program. Variables act as placeholders for information, enabling dynamic and reusable programming.

Syntax:

```
x = 5
y = "Hello, World!"
```

Syntax Explanation:

- `x = 5`: Assigns the integer 5 to the variable x, which can be used in mathematical operations or logic.
- `y = "Hello, World!"`: Assigns the string to the variable y, which can be printed, concatenated, or manipulated.
- Variables in Python are dynamically typed, meaning their type can change based on the value assigned.
- Variables can also store complex data types like lists, dictionaries, or custom objects, making them versatile tools in programming.

Example:

```
# Assign values to variables
x = 10
y = "Python Basics"
z = x * 2
print(x, y, z)
```

Example Explanation:

- Outputs: `10 Python Basics 20`
- Demonstrates variable assignment, manipulation, and usage in expressions.

2. Use Lists

What is Use Lists?

A list is a collection of items that are ordered and can be modified, allowing for dynamic data storage and manipulation. It supports duplicate elements and can store items of different data types, making it a flexible choice for various programming tasks.

Syntax:

```
my_list = [1, 2, 3]
```

Syntax Explanation:

- `my_list`: Creates a list containing integers.
- Lists can grow or shrink dynamically, enabling efficient addition or removal of elements.
- They can store any data type, including numbers, strings, or even other lists, offering high flexibility.
- Common operations include slicing, appending, and iterating over items.

Example:

```
# Create and manipulate a list
my_list = ["apple", "banana", "cherry"]
my_list.append("date")
my_list.remove("banana")
print(my_list)
```

Example Explanation:

- Adds "date" to the list and removes "banana".
- Outputs: `['apple', 'cherry', 'date']`

- Highlights list mutability and common operations like adding and removing elements.

3. Write a Function

What is Write a Function?

Defines reusable blocks of code designed to perform specific tasks, making programs more organized, efficient, and easier to maintain. Functions encapsulate logic, allowing the same code to be executed multiple times with different inputs, reducing redundancy and enhancing readability.

Syntax:

```
def my_function():
    print("Hello, World!")
```

Syntax Explanation:

- def: Keyword to define a function.
- my_function(): The function name, which should describe its purpose.
- Functions can accept parameters and return values, increasing their flexibility.
- A well-designed function focuses on a single task, adhering to the principle of modularity.

Example:

```
# Define and call a function
def greet(name):
    return f"Hello, {name}!"

print(greet("Alice"))
print(greet("Bob"))
```

Example Explanation:

- Outputs: Hello, Alice!
  Hello, Bob!
- Demonstrates how functions can accept arguments and return values.

4. Loop Through Data
What is Loop Through Data?
Iterates over elements in a collection, such as a list or tuple, allowing each item to be accessed and manipulated in sequence. This makes it possible to perform repetitive tasks, such as calculations or printing, on all elements of the collection efficiently.

Syntax:
```
for item in my_list:
    print(item)
```

Syntax Explanation:
- `for item in my_list:` Iterates through each element in the list, assigning it to the variable `item` for each iteration.
- Loops can work with any iterable, including strings, tuples, dictionaries, and sets.
- Nested loops allow iterating through complex structures, like lists of lists.

Example:
```
# Loop through a list
fruits = ["apple", "banana", "cherry"]
for fruit in fruits:
    print(f"I like {fruit}.")
```

Example Explanation:
- Outputs each fruit with a custom message: `I like apple.`
  `I like banana.`
  `I like cherry.`
- Demonstrates how loops integrate with string formatting for dynamic outputs.

5. Import Libraries
What is Import Libraries?
Imports external Python libraries to extend the core functionality of Python, enabling specialized operations like data analysis, visualization, machine learning, and more. Libraries provide pre-built tools and functions, saving time and enhancing productivity for developers.

Syntax:
```
import pandas as pd
```
Syntax Explanation:
- import pandas: Loads the Pandas library, adding its extensive data manipulation capabilities to your program.
- as pd: Provides a convenient alias to simplify repeated use of the library's name.
- Libraries enable developers to focus on higher-level problems by abstracting complex functionality.

Example:
```
# Import Pandas and create a DataFrame
import pandas as pd
data = {"Name": ["Alice", "Bob"], "Age": [25, 30]}
df = pd.DataFrame(data)
print(df)
```
Example Explanation:
- Creates a DataFrame using Pandas.
- Outputs: Name   Age
  0   Alice   25
  1   Bob   30
- Highlights how external libraries like Pandas simplify data manipulation tasks.

Real-Life Project:
Project Name: Simple Data Aggregator
Project Goal:
Write a Python program that calculates the average value from a list of numbers.
Code for This Project:
```
# Define a function to calculate the average
def calculate_average(numbers):
    return sum(numbers) / len(numbers)
# Use the function on a sample list
sample_data = [10, 20, 30, 40, 50]
average = calculate_average(sample_data)
print(f"The average is: {average}")
```

Expanded Features:
- Combines function definition and list usage.
- Demonstrates Python basics applied to a practical task.
- Shows how to handle numerical data dynamically.

Expected Output:
```
The average is: 30.0
```

Chapter-3 Getting Started with Pandas

Pandas is a powerful Python library for data manipulation and analysis. It provides high-performance data structures like Series and DataFrame, making it essential for handling structured data efficiently. This chapter introduces the fundamental concepts of Pandas, helping you get started with loading, manipulating, and analyzing data.

Key Characteristics of Pandas:
- **Easy Data Handling:** Simplifies operations like filtering, grouping, and reshaping data.
- **Flexible Data Structures:** Includes Series (1D) and DataFrame (2D) for data representation.
- **Integration:** Works seamlessly with other Python libraries like NumPy and Matplotlib.
- **Rich Functionality:** Provides extensive methods for data cleaning, transformation, and analysis.
- **File Handling:** Supports reading and writing data in various formats like CSV, Excel, and SQL.

Basic Rules for Using Pandas:
1. Install Pandas using pip install pandas.
2. Import the library in your script or notebook with import pandas as pd.
3. Create or load data into Pandas structures like Series and DataFrame.
4. Use Pandas methods for data manipulation and analysis.
5. Visualize insights using integrated or external plotting libraries.

Best Practices:

- **Understand Data Structures:** Know when to use Series versus DataFrame.
- **Handle Missing Data:** Use methods like fillna() or dropna() effectively.
- **Optimize Memory Usage:** Convert data types to reduce memory consumption.
- **Leverage Vectorized Operations:** Use Pandas' built-in methods instead of loops for efficiency.
- **Explore Data Thoroughly:** Use methods like info() and describe() to understand the dataset.

Syntax Table:

SL No	Concept	Syntax/Example	Description
1	Import Pandas	`import pandas as pd`	Loads the Pandas library.
2	Create a Series	`pd.Series([1, 2, 3])`	Creates a one-dimensional array.
3	Create a DataFrame	`pd.DataFrame(data)`	Creates a two-dimensional table.
4	Read CSV File	`pd.read_csv('file.csv')`	Loads data from a CSV file.
5	Basic Statistics	`df.describe()`	Summarizes statistics for numerical data.

Syntax Explanation:

1. Import Pandas

What is Import Pandas?

Imports the Pandas library, providing access to its powerful data manipulation and analysis tools.

Syntax:
```
import pandas as pd
```
Syntax Explanation:

- import pandas: Loads the Pandas library into your Python environment.
- as pd: Assigns the alias pd for convenient access to Pandas functions and methods.
- Importing Pandas is the first step to accessing its data handling capabilities, such as creating DataFrames or reading files.
- Once imported, you can seamlessly integrate Pandas with other libraries like Matplotlib or NumPy for extended functionality.

Example:
```
# Import Pandas library
import pandas as pd
```

Example Explanation:

- After importing, you can use pd to call Pandas functions like pd.DataFrame() or pd.read_csv().

2. Create a Series

What is Create a Series?
A Series is a one-dimensional labeled array capable of holding any data type, such as integers, floats, strings, or even other objects. Each element in the Series is associated with a unique index, making it ideal for handling data with a meaningful order or labels.

Syntax:
```
pd.Series([1, 2, 3])
```

Syntax Explanation:

- pd.Series(): Constructs a Pandas Series from a list, array, or scalar value.
- Elements in a Series are automatically assigned an index starting at 0 unless specified.

- Series provide fast access to elements using their index, enabling efficient data retrieval and manipulation.
- They can be used to represent time-series data or any linear sequence of values.

Example:

```
# Create a Pandas Series
data = pd.Series([10, 20, 30], index=["A", "B", "C"])
print(data)
```

Example Explanation:

- Outputs:
```
A    10
B    20
C    30
dtype: int64
```
- Assigns custom indices A, B, and C to the Series, demonstrating its labeled structure.

3. Create a DataFrame

What is Create a DataFrame?
A DataFrame is a two-dimensional, size-mutable, and heterogeneous tabular data structure, meaning it can hold data of different types (e.g., numeric, string, boolean) and allows for dynamic modification of rows and columns. It is similar to a spreadsheet or SQL table and is one of Pandas' most powerful features for organizing and analyzing structured data.
Syntax:
```
pd.DataFrame(data)
```

Syntax Explanation:
- pd.DataFrame(data): Creates a DataFrame from various data structures like dictionaries, lists, or NumPy arrays.
- DataFrames have labeled rows and columns, enabling intuitive access and manipulation of data.
- They support a wide range of operations like filtering, sorting, and aggregation.

- You can specify column names and row indices explicitly or let Pandas generate default labels.

Example:
```
# Create a Pandas DataFrame
data = {"Name": ["Alice", "Bob"], "Age": [25, 30]}
df = pd.DataFrame(data, index=["Row1", "Row2"])
print(df)
```

Example Explanation:

- Outputs:
  ```
              Name  Age
  Row1  Alice   25
  Row2    Bob   30
  ```

- Custom row indices Row1 and Row2 enhance readability and accessibility.

4. Read CSV File

What is Read CSV File?
Loads data from a CSV file into a Pandas DataFrame for analysis, providing an easy and efficient way to handle structured data. This method is ideal for datasets with tabular structures, such as those commonly used in data analysis and reporting workflows.

Syntax:
```
pd.read_csv('file.csv')
```

Syntax Explanation:

- pd.read_csv('file.csv'): Reads the CSV file and converts it into a DataFrame.
- Automatically infers column names and data types from the file.
- Additional parameters allow customization, such as specifying delimiters (sep), handling headers (header), or setting an index column (index_col).
- Efficiently handles large datasets, making it a preferred choice for data ingestion.

Example:

```
# Load data from a CSV file
df = pd.read_csv('data.csv')
print(df.head())
```

Example Explanation:

- Displays the first few rows of the loaded DataFrame using head() for quick inspection.

5. Basic Statistics

What is Basic Statistics?
Provides a comprehensive summary of numerical data in a DataFrame, including metrics like count, mean, standard deviation, minimum, and maximum values, as well as percentiles. These statistics help in understanding the distribution, central tendency, and variability of the dataset.

Syntax:
```
df.describe()
```

Syntax Explanation:

- df.describe(): Computes summary statistics like mean, standard deviation, min, and max for numerical columns.
- Offers a quick overview of the dataset's key characteristics, aiding in initial data exploration.
- For categorical columns, the method can include counts, unique values, top occurrences, and frequency if include='all' is specified.

Example:

```
# Compute summary statistics
summary = df.describe()
print(summary)
```

Example Explanation:
- Outputs: Age

  count   2.0
  mean   27.5
  std   3.5
  min   25.0
  25%   26.25
  50%   27.5
  75%   28.75
  max   30.0

- Summarizes the statistics of the Age column, highlighting its distribution and central tendency.

Real-Life Project:

Project Name: Basic Data Inspection and Analysis

Project Goal:
Load a dataset, inspect its structure, and compute summary statistics to understand its contents.

Code for This Project:

```python
# Import Pandas and load data
import pandas as pd

data = {
    "Name": ["Alice", "Bob", "Charlie"],
    "Age": [25, 30, 35],
    "Salary": [50000, 60000, 70000]
}
df = pd.DataFrame(data)
# Inspect the dataset
print("DataFrame Info:")
print(df.info())
print("\nSummary Statistics:")
print(df.describe())
```

Expanded Features:

- Combines data loading and inspection.
- Demonstrates the use of info() and describe() for dataset exploration.
- Prepares the dataset for further analysis or cleaning.

Expected Output:

DataFrame Info:

```
<class 'pandas.core.frame.DataFrame'>
RangeIndex: 3 entries, 0 to 2
Data columns (total 3 columns):
 #   Column  Non-Null Count  Dtype
---  ------  --------------  -----
 0   Name    3 non-null      object
 1   Age     3 non-null      int64
 2   Salary  3 non-null      int64
dtypes: int64(2), object(1)
memory usage: 200.0+ bytes


Summary Statistics:
             Age         Salary
count   3.000000       3.000000
mean   30.000000   60000.000000
std     5.000000   10000.000000
min    25.000000   50000.000000
25%    27.500000   55000.000000
50%    30.000000   60000.000000
75%    32.500000   65000.000000
max    35.000000   70000.000000
```

Chapter-4 Creating Series and DataFrames in Pandas

Pandas provides two primary data structures: Series and DataFrame. These are fundamental for data manipulation and analysis. This chapter explores how to create Series and DataFrames, understand their structure, and populate them with data from various sources like lists, dictionaries, and external files.

Key Characteristics of Series and DataFrames:

- **Series:** A one-dimensional labeled array that can hold any data type (e.g., integers, strings, floats).
- **DataFrame:** A two-dimensional labeled data structure, similar to a spreadsheet or SQL table, capable of holding multiple data types in different columns.
- **Flexible Construction:** Can be created from lists, dictionaries, NumPy arrays, or directly from raw data files.
- **Indexing and Labeling:** Both structures allow labeled rows and columns for easy data access.
- **Integration:** Compatible with other Python libraries like NumPy and Matplotlib.

Basic Rules for Creating Series and DataFrames:

1. Use `pd.Series()` for creating one-dimensional arrays.
2. Use `pd.DataFrame()` for creating tabular, two-dimensional data.
3. Specify an `index` parameter for custom labels.
4. Ensure data consistency in columns when constructing DataFrames.
5. Convert other data structures (e.g., lists, dictionaries) into Series or DataFrames as needed.

Best Practices:

- **Use Explicit Indexing:** Assign meaningful index labels to make data interpretation easier.
- **Handle Missing Data:** Use NaN for missing entries and handle them appropriately.
- **Combine Data Sources:** Merge or concatenate multiple Series or

DataFrames for comprehensive analysis.

- **Document Data Origin:** Maintain clear metadata about how the data was sourced and processed.
- **Start Small:** Begin with small, manually-created Series or DataFrames for practice before working with large datasets.

Syntax Table:

SL No	Concept	Syntax/Example	Description
1	Create a Series	`pd.Series([1, 2, 3])`	Creates a one-dimensional array.
2	Create a Series with Index	`pd.Series([1, 2, 3], index=['a', 'b', 'c'])`	Creates a Series with custom indices.
3	Create a DataFrame from Dict	`pd.DataFrame({'A': [1, 2], 'B': [3, 4]})`	Creates a DataFrame from a dictionary.
4	Create a DataFrame from List	`pd.DataFrame([[1, 2], [3, 4]], columns=['A', 'B'])`	Creates a DataFrame from a list of lists.
5	Create an Empty DataFrame	`pd.DataFrame(columns=['A', 'B'])`	Creates an empty DataFrame.

Syntax Explanation:

1. Create a Series

What is Create a Series?

A Series is a one-dimensional labeled array capable of holding any data type. It is ideal for storing simple sequences of values with optional labeling.

Syntax:

`pd.Series([1, 2, 3])`

Syntax Explanation:

- `pd.Series([1, 2, 3])`: Creates a Series from a list of integers.
- The default index is integer-based, starting from 0.

- The Series can store various data types, including integers, floats, strings, and objects.
- Each element in the Series is associated with an index, which can be used to retrieve or manipulate specific values efficiently.
- The Series structure supports vectorized operations, enabling quick mathematical or logical transformations.

Example:
```
# Create a Pandas Series
data = pd.Series([100, 200, 300])
print(data)
```

Example Explanation:
- Outputs: 0   100
  - 1   200
  - 2   300
  - dtype: int64
- Demonstrates default indexing and integer values.
- Highlights the data type (int64) and the ability to operate on numerical data.

2. Create a Series with Index

What is Create a Series with Index?
Assigns custom labels to the elements of a Series, making it easier to reference and interpret data.

Syntax:
```
pd.Series([1, 2, 3], index=['a', 'b', 'c'])
```

Syntax Explanation:
- index=['a', 'b', 'c']: Specifies custom labels for the Series elements.
- The labels allow for non-numeric indexing and better data organization.
- Custom indices can represent meaningful identifiers, such as dates, categories, or names.
- The flexibility of labeling enhances the interpretability of the Series when used in analysis or visualization.

Example:
```
# Create a Series with custom indices
data = pd.Series([10, 20, 30], index=['x', 'y', 'z'])
print(data)
```
Example Explanation:

- Outputs: x   10
  y   20
  z   30
  dtype: int64

- Displays the Series with custom indices.
- Highlights how meaningful labels improve clarity and usability.

3. Create a DataFrame from Dict

What is Create a DataFrame from Dict?
A common way to create a DataFrame by mapping column names to lists of values.
Syntax:
```
pd.DataFrame({'A': [1, 2], 'B': [3, 4]})
```

Syntax Explanation:

- Keys in the dictionary ('A', 'B') become column names.
- Values in the dictionary (lists [1, 2], [3, 4]) populate the columns.
- DataFrames created this way are easy to construct programmatically.
- The dictionary structure ensures each column is independent and can be manipulated without affecting others.
- Supports heterogeneous data types across columns, allowing for diverse data representation.

Example:
```
# Create a DataFrame from a dictionary
data = {'Name': ['Alice', 'Bob'], 'Age': [25, 30]}
df = pd.DataFrame(data)
```

```
print(df)
```

Example Explanation:
- Outputs: Name   Age
  ```
  0   Alice   25
  1     Bob   30
  ```
- Maps the dictionary keys to column headers and lists to column values.
- Ensures structured and labeled representation of data.

4. Create a DataFrame from List

What is Create a DataFrame from List?
Constructs a DataFrame from a list of lists, where each inner list represents a row.

Syntax:
```
pd.DataFrame([[1, 2], [3, 4]], columns=['A', 'B'])
```

Syntax Explanation:
- [[1, 2], [3, 4]]: Defines rows of the DataFrame.
- columns=['A', 'B']: Assigns column labels to the DataFrame.
- This method is useful for creating small DataFrames manually.
- The row-based construction is intuitive when data naturally aligns with rows, such as in matrices.
- Each column can be accessed or manipulated individually, enabling flexibility.

Example:
```
# Create a DataFrame from a list of lists
data = [[100, 'A'], [200, 'B']]
df = pd.DataFrame(data, columns=['Value', 'Category'])
print(df)
```

Example Explanation:
- Outputs: Value Category
  ```
  0     100        A
  1     200        B
  ```
- Rows and columns are explicitly defined, showcasing flexibility.

- Highlights the assignment of labels for better data interpretation.

5. Create an Empty DataFrame

What is Create an Empty DataFrame?
Creates an empty DataFrame with specified column names, useful as a template for populating data dynamically.
Syntax:
```
pd.DataFrame(columns=['A', 'B'])
```

Syntax Explanation:
- `columns=['A', 'B']`: Defines column headers without assigning any data.
- Creates a structure ready for inserting data later.
- Useful for initializing DataFrames for iterative or programmatic data population.
- Provides a flexible starting point for dynamic data manipulation.

Example:
```
# Create an empty DataFrame
df = pd.DataFrame(columns=['ID', 'Name', 'Score'])
print(df)
```

Example Explanation:
- Outputs: `Empty DataFrame`
  `Columns: [ID, Name, Score]`
  `Index: []`
- Displays an empty DataFrame structure.
- Demonstrates how to define columns in advance while leaving rows to be added later.

Real-Life Project:

Project Name: Dynamic DataFrame Construction
Project Goal:
Create and populate a DataFrame with student scores dynamically.

Code for This Project:
```python
import pandas as pd

# Initialize an empty DataFrame
data = pd.DataFrame(columns=['Student', 'Subject',
'Score'])

# Populate the DataFrame
data = data.append({'Student': 'Alice', 'Subject':
'Math', 'Score': 95}, ignore_index=True)
data = data.append({'Student': 'Bob', 'Subject':
'Science', 'Score': 88}, ignore_index=True)

print(data)
```
Expanded Features:
- Demonstrates dynamic creation and population of DataFrames.
- Highlights how to append rows to an empty DataFrame.
- Explains the importance of `ignore_index` for proper row indexing during appending.

Expected Output:
```
  Student  Subject  Score
0   Alice     Math     95
1     Bob  Science     88
```

Chapter-5 Indexing and Slicing in Pandas

Indexing and slicing are essential for accessing and manipulating data in Pandas. These operations allow you to select specific rows, columns, or elements from Series and DataFrames efficiently. This chapter provides an in-depth guide to mastering indexing and slicing techniques, ensuring effective data manipulation.

Key Characteristics of Indexing and Slicing:

- **Row and Column Access:** Enables selection of specific rows and columns using labels or positions.
- **Boolean Indexing:** Filters data based on conditions.
- **Hierarchical Indexing:** Works with multi-level indices for complex data structures.
- **Flexible Slicing:** Supports a variety of slicing techniques for rows and columns.
- **Integration:** Combines well with other Pandas functions for seamless workflows.

Basic Rules for Indexing and Slicing:

1. Use `.loc[]` for label-based indexing and slicing.
2. Use `.iloc[]` for position-based indexing and slicing.
3. Boolean indexing requires a condition that evaluates to a Boolean array.
4. Multi-level indexing requires specifying levels or using tuples for precise access.
5. Avoid chaining operations for complex selections; use `.loc[]` or `.iloc[]` explicitly.

Best Practices:

- **Understand Index Types:** Know the difference between positional and label-based indexing.
- **Handle Missing Indices:** Use methods like `.reset_index()` to standardize indices.
- **Avoid Ambiguity:** Use `.loc[]` and `.iloc[]` explicitly to prevent confusion.
- **Document Filters:** Maintain clarity by commenting on slicing logic.
- **Test Selections:** Verify slices on small datasets before applying to

large ones.

Syntax Table:

SL	Technique	Syntax/Example	Description
1	Access Row by Label	`df.loc['row_label']`	Selects a row by its label.
2	Access Row by Position	`df.iloc[0]`	Selects a row by its position.
3	Select Multiple Columns	`df[['col1', 'col2']]`	Selects multiple columns by their names.
4	Boolean Indexing	`df[df['col'] > value]`	Filters rows based on a condition.
5	Slice Rows	`df[1:4]`	Slices rows by position.

Syntax Explanation:

1. Access Row by Label

What is Access Row by Label?
Selects a specific row from a DataFrame using its label.
Syntax:
`df.loc['row_label']`

Syntax Explanation:
- `df.loc[]`: Accesses rows and columns by labels.
- `'row_label'`: The label of the row to select.
- Can also select a range of rows by label, e.g., `df.loc['label1':'label2']`.
- Ensures precise selection, especially for non-numeric indices.

Example:
```
import pandas as pd
# Create a DataFrame
data = {'A': [1, 2, 3], 'B': [4, 5, 6]}
df = pd.DataFrame(data, index=['row1', 'row2', 'row3'])
print(df.loc['row1'])
```

Example Explanation:

- Outputs: A   1

       B   4

  `Name: row1, dtype: int64`
- Selects the first row using its label.

2. Access Row by Position

What is Access Row by Position?

Selects a specific row from a DataFrame using its position.

Syntax:

`df.iloc[0]`

Syntax Explanation:

- `df.iloc[]`: Accesses rows and columns by integer positions.
- `0`: Refers to the first row (0-based indexing).
- Supports slicing for multiple rows, e.g., `df.iloc[0:2]`.

Example:

```
# Access the first row by position
print(df.iloc[0])
```

Example Explanation:

- Outputs: A   1

       B   4

  `Name: row1, dtype: int64`
- Selects the first row using its position.

3. Select Multiple Columns

What is Select Multiple Columns?

Extracts multiple columns from a DataFrame using their names.

Syntax:

`df[['col1', 'col2']]`

Syntax Explanation:

- `[['col1', 'col2']]`: Passes a list of column names to select multiple columns.
- Ensures that only the specified columns are returned.

Example:
```
# Select columns A and B
print(df[['A', 'B']])
```
Example Explanation:
- Outputs: A   B
  ```
  row1   1   4
  row2   2   5
  row3   3   6
  ```
- Selects both columns A and B.

4. Boolean Indexing

What is Boolean Indexing?
Filters rows based on a condition.
Syntax:
```
df[df['col'] > value]
```

Syntax Explanation:
- df['col'] > value: Evaluates a condition for each element in the column.
- Returns a Boolean array used to filter rows.
- Can combine multiple conditions with & (and) or | (or).

Example:
```
# Filter rows where column A > 1
filtered = df[df['A'] > 1]
print(filtered)
```
Example Explanation:
- Outputs: A   B
  ```
  row2   2   5
  row3   3   6
  ```
- Filters rows where the value in column A is greater than 1.

5. Slice Rows

What is Slice Rows?
Selects a range of rows by their position.
Syntax:
df[1:4]
Syntax Explanation:
- df[1:4]: Slices rows from position 1 to 3 (excludes the stop index).
- Supports step values for skipping rows, e.g., df[::2].
- Best used for quick, simple slicing tasks.

Example:
```
# Slice rows by position
sliced = df[1:3]
print(sliced)
```
Example Explanation:
- Outputs: A   B
    row2   2   5
    row3   3   6
- Selects rows from position 1 to 2.

Real-Life Project:

Project Name: Sales Data Filtering
Project Goal:
Filter and analyze a dataset to extract high-performing sales regions.
Code for This Project:
```
import pandas as pd
# Sample sales data
data = {
    'Region': ['North', 'South', 'East', 'West'],
    'Sales': [300, 150, 400, 250]
}
df = pd.DataFrame(data)
# Filter regions with sales above 200
high_sales = df[df['Sales'] > 200]
print(high_sales)
```

Expanded Features:

- Demonstrates filtering with Boolean indexing.
- Highlights column-based condition evaluation.
- Provides actionable insights from the dataset.

Expected Output:

```
  Region  Sales
0  North    300
2   East    400
3   West    250
```

Part 2: Essential Operations

Chapter-6 Basic DataFrame Operations in Pandas

This chapter explores fundamental operations on Pandas DataFrames, a versatile data structure for handling and analyzing tabular data in Python. Understanding these basic operations is key to data manipulation and preprocessing for analysis and machine learning tasks.

Key Characteristics of DataFrame Operations:

- **Flexibility:** Provides numerous methods for selecting, modifying, and analyzing data.
- **Ease of Use:** Offers intuitive syntax for performing complex operations.
- **Scalability:** Efficiently handles both small and large datasets.
- **Integration:** Works seamlessly with NumPy, Matplotlib, and other Python libraries.
- **Versatility:** Supports various data formats and complex data manipulations.

Basic Rules for DataFrame Operations:

- Operations can be performed on rows, columns, or individual elements.
- DataFrame methods return new objects or modify data in place based on the method used.
- Labels and indices provide flexibility for selecting and modifying data.
- Operations are vectorized, making them faster than manual loops.

Best Practices:

- **Use Vectorized Operations:** Leverage built-in Pandas methods for efficiency.
- **Validate Data Types:** Check column data types using `df.dtypes` for compatibility.

- **Chain Operations:** Combine multiple methods for concise and effective code.
- **Handle Missing Data:** Use df.fillna() or df.dropna() for missing value treatment.
- **Leverage Indexing:** Use loc and iloc for precise row and column selection.

Syntax Table:

SL No	Function/Feature	Syntax/Example	Description
1	Column Selection	df['column_name']	Selects a specific column.
2	Row Selection	df.loc[label] or df.iloc[index]	Selects a specific row by label or index.
3	Filtering Rows	df[df['column'] > value]	Filters rows based on conditions.
4	Adding a Column	df['new_column'] = data	Adds a new column to the DataFrame.
5	Summary Statistics	df.describe()	Computes summary statistics.

Syntax Explanation:

1. Column Selection

What is Column Selection?
Allows selecting specific columns from the DataFrame for further analysis. Column selection can be seamlessly combined with operations like filtering, grouping, and computation, enabling powerful and concise data manipulation.

Syntax:
df['column_name']

Syntax Explanation:
- df: The DataFrame object.
- 'column_name': The name of the column to select.
- Returns a Series object representing the selected column.
- Multiple columns can be selected using a list: df[['col1',

'col2']].

- Column selection is often used in conjunction with filtering and computation to isolate specific data subsets for targeted analysis.

Example:
```
import pandas as pd
# Create a DataFrame
data = {'Name': ['Alice', 'Bob', 'Charlie'], 'Age':
[25, 30, 35]}
df = pd.DataFrame(data)
# Select the 'Name' column
names = df['Name']
print("Names:", names)
```

Example Explanation:
- Creates a DataFrame with columns Name and Age.
- Selects the Name column, returning a Series object: ['Alice', 'Bob', 'Charlie'].
- Column selection simplifies focusing on specific data dimensions for detailed analysis.

2. Row Selection

What is Row Selection?
Allows selecting specific rows by label or index, providing flexibility for precise data extraction and enabling advanced operations such as row-specific transformations or condition-based filtering.

Syntax:
```
df.loc[label]
# or
df.iloc[index]
```

Syntax Explanation:
- loc: Selects rows by their label.
- iloc: Selects rows by their integer index.
- Both return a Series or DataFrame, depending on the input.
- Row selection is particularly useful when applying modifications or analysis to a subset of rows based on their position or label.

Example:
```
# Select the row with index 1
row = df.iloc[1]
print("Row:", row)
```

Example Explanation:
- Selects the second row (index 1) of the DataFrame, returning `Name: Bob, Age: 30`.
- Row selection facilitates detailed inspections or transformations of individual records.

3. Filtering Rows

What is Filtering Rows?
Filters rows based on conditions applied to column values. This operation is crucial for isolating specific subsets of data that meet particular criteria, enabling targeted analysis or transformations. It allows dynamic row selection by applying conditions directly to columns, streamlining workflows in data preprocessing and exploration.

Syntax:
```
df[df['column'] > value]
```

Syntax Explanation:
- Evaluates the condition on the specified column.
- Returns a filtered DataFrame with rows that satisfy the condition.
- Filtering rows is often the first step in cleaning or refining datasets for focused analysis.

Example:
```
# Filter rows where Age > 25
filtered = df[df['Age'] > 25]
print("Filtered DataFrame:", filtered)
```

Example Explanation:
- Filters rows where the Age column has values greater than 25.
- Outputs rows for Bob and Charlie.
- Filtering simplifies isolating relevant data for specific analytical

tasks.

4. Adding a Column

What is Adding a Column?
Adds a new column to the DataFrame, enabling not only the integration of calculated values or external data but also allowing for dynamic expansion of the dataset to support advanced analysis and feature engineering.
Syntax:
```
df['new_column'] = data
```

Syntax Explanation:
- new_column: The name of the column to add.
- data: List, Series, or array containing values for the new column.
- Adding columns is integral to enriching datasets with new attributes derived from existing data or external inputs.

Example:
```
# Add a 'Salary' column
df['Salary'] = [50000, 60000, 70000]
print("Updated DataFrame:", df)
```

Example Explanation:
- Adds a Salary column with values [50000, 60000, 70000].
- Updates the DataFrame to include the new column.
- Adding columns supports feature creation for machine learning workflows or enhancing datasets with additional information.

5. Summary Statistics

What is Summary Statistics?
Computes descriptive statistics for numeric columns, providing a quick overview of key metrics such as count, mean, standard deviation, minimum, maximum, and quartile values. This operation is invaluable for understanding the distribution and variability of data at a glance, aiding in both exploratory data analysis and decision-making.

Syntax:
```
df.describe()
```

Syntax Explanation:
- Analyzes numeric columns in the DataFrame.
- Computes count, mean, standard deviation, min, max, and quartiles.
- Summary statistics are foundational for identifying patterns, detecting anomalies, and preparing data for further analysis.

Example:
```
# Get summary statistics
stats = df.describe()
print("Summary Statistics:\n", stats)
```

Example Explanation:
- Outputs a summary of the numeric Age and Salary columns.
- Includes mean, min, max, and other statistics.
- Summary statistics enable quick diagnostics of data properties, helping shape analysis strategies.

Real-Life Project:

Project Name: Employee Data Analysis
Project Goal:
Analyze employee data to extract insights, such as identifying employees above a certain age and computing average salaries.
Code for This Project:
```
import pandas as pd
# Create a DataFrame
employee_data = {
    'Name': ['Alice', 'Bob', 'Charlie', 'David'],
    'Age': [25, 30, 35, 40],
    'Salary': [50000, 60000, 70000, 80000]
}
df = pd.DataFrame(employee_data)

# Filter employees older than 30
```

```python
older_employees = df[df['Age'] > 30]
print("Employees older than 30:\n", older_employees)

# Compute the average salary
average_salary = df['Salary'].mean()
print("Average Salary:", average_salary)
```

Expanded Features:
- Filters rows based on conditions for targeted analysis.
- Computes summary statistics for key insights.
- Demonstrates adding and modifying columns dynamically.

Expected Output:

Employees older than 30:

```
      Name  Age  Salary
2  Charlie   35   70000
3    David   40   80000
```

Average Salary:

```
65000.0
```

This project highlights practical use of basic DataFrame operations for efficient data analysis.

Chapter-7 Working with Missing Data in Pandas

Handling missing data is a critical aspect of data preprocessing and analysis. Pandas offers robust tools to detect, analyze, and manage missing values, ensuring that datasets are clean and suitable for further processing. This chapter delves into the methods and best practices for effectively working with missing data in Pandas.

Key Characteristics of Handling Missing Data in Pandas:

- **Detection:** Identify missing values efficiently with built-in methods.
- **Flexibility:** Provides multiple strategies for handling missing values, such as removal or imputation.
- **Integration:** Works seamlessly with other Pandas operations and libraries like NumPy.
- **Customization:** Allows users to define and manage their missing value indicators.
- **Performance:** Optimized for large datasets, ensuring efficient handling of missing data.

Basic Rules for Handling Missing Data:

1. Missing values in Pandas are represented as NaN (Not a Number) for numeric data and None for object data types.
2. Operations on missing values typically result in NaN unless explicitly handled.
3. Methods such as `dropna()` or `fillna()` can be used to manage missing values.
4. Detect missing values using functions like `isnull()` and `notnull()`.

Best Practices:

- **Understand Data:** Assess the extent and pattern of missing values before applying transformations.
- **Choose the Right Strategy:** Decide whether to drop, fill, or interpolate missing values based on the data context.
- **Avoid Data Loss:** Use imputation or advanced modeling techniques where dropping data may lead to significant

information loss.
- **Validate After Handling:** Check the dataset after handling missing values to ensure consistency.
- **Leverage Visualization:** Use visual tools like heatmaps to understand the distribution of missing data.

Syntax Table:

SL No	Function/Feature	Syntax/Example	Description
1	Detect Missing Values	df.isnull()	Identifies missing values in the DataFrame.
2	Remove Missing Values	df.dropna()	Drops rows or columns with missing values.
3	Fill Missing Values	df.fillna(value)	Replaces missing values with a specified value.
4	Interpolate Missing Values	df.interpolate()	Estimates missing values using interpolation.
5	Count Missing Values	df.isnull().sum()	Counts missing values for each column.

Syntax Explanation:

1. Detect Missing Values

What is Detect Missing Values?
Detects missing values in the DataFrame, returning a Boolean DataFrame where True indicates a missing value.

Syntax:
df.isnull()

Syntax Explanation:
- df: The input DataFrame to analyze for missing values.
- Returns a DataFrame of the same shape, with True for missing values and False for non-missing values.

- Missing values are typically represented as NaN in numeric columns and None in object or string columns.
- Useful for visualizing the pattern of missing data and identifying problematic areas in the dataset.
- This method can be combined with further operations like sum() to aggregate results for each column.
- Essential for preparing data before applying transformations or imputations.

Example:
```
import pandas as pd
# Create a DataFrame
data = {'Name': ['Alice', 'Bob', None], 'Age': [25, None, 35]}
df = pd.DataFrame(data)
missing_values = df.isnull()
print("Missing Values:\n", missing_values)
```

Example Explanation:
- Creates a DataFrame with missing values in Name and Age columns.
- Outputs a Boolean DataFrame indicating missing values: Name Age
  ```
  0  False  False
  1  False   True
  2   True  False
  ```

- This output can guide further processing, such as replacing or dropping missing values.

2. Remove Missing Values

What is Remove Missing Values?
Drops rows or columns containing missing values from the DataFrame.
Syntax:
```
df.dropna(axis=0, how='any')
```

Syntax Explanation:

- `axis=0`: Drops rows by default. Use `axis=1` to drop columns.
- `how='any'`: Drops rows/columns if any value is missing. Use `how='all'` to drop only if all values are missing.
- `thresh`: Optional parameter to specify a minimum number of non-NA values required to retain a row or column.
- Returns a new DataFrame with the specified rows or columns removed, leaving the original DataFrame unchanged unless `inplace=True` is specified.
- Ideal for quickly cleaning datasets with scattered missing values in non-critical columns or rows.
- Use cautiously to avoid unintentional data loss in datasets with significant missing values.

Example:
```
cleaned_df = df.dropna()
print("DataFrame after dropping missing values:\n",
cleaned_df)
```

Example Explanation:

- Removes rows with missing values.
- Outputs: Name   Age
  0   Alice   25.0
- Dropping missing values is suitable when the proportion of missing data is small, and its removal doesn't significantly affect the analysis.

3. Fill Missing Values

What is Fill Missing Values?
Replaces missing values with a specified value or method, such as forward-fill or backward-fill.

Syntax:
```
df.fillna(value, method=None)
```

Syntax Explanation:

- `value`: The replacement value for missing data, which can be a scalar, dictionary, or Series.

- method: Specifies a fill method ('ffill' for forward-fill, 'bfill' for backward-fill), prioritizing adjacent values for imputation.
- axis: Determines whether to fill missing values row-wise or column-wise. Default is column-wise.
- inplace: Modifies the DataFrame in place if set to True.
- Returns a new DataFrame or modifies the original DataFrame based on the inplace parameter.
- Filling missing values is especially useful for preparing datasets for algorithms that cannot handle null entries.
- Enables the preservation of dataset structure while addressing gaps in the data.

Example:
```
filled_df = df.fillna({'Name': 'Unknown', 'Age':
df['Age'].mean()})
print("DataFrame after filling missing values:\n",
filled_df)
```

Example Explanation:
- Fills missing Name values with 'Unknown'.
- Replaces missing Age values with the column mean.
- Outputs: Name   Age
  ```
  0  Alice   25.0
  1    Bob   30.0
  2  Unknown 35.0
  ```
- This method balances data retention and integrity by imputing meaningful values.

4. Interpolate Missing Values

What is Interpolate Missing Values?
Estimates and fills missing values using interpolation methods.
Syntax:
```
df.interpolate(method='linear')
```

Syntax Explanation:

- method: Specifies the interpolation method (`'linear'` by default, with options like `'polynomial'` or `'spline'`).
- limit: Limits the number of consecutive NaNs to fill.
- limit_direction: Controls whether filling is forward (`'forward'`), backward (`'backward'`), or both (`'both'`).
- Suitable for numeric data where values are missing in a sequence, maintaining continuity in trends.
- Preserves natural patterns in data, particularly for time-series or sequential datasets.

Example:

```
interpolated_df = df.interpolate()
print("DataFrame after interpolation:\n",
interpolated_df)
```

Example Explanation:

- Interpolates missing Age values using linear interpolation.
- Outputs a DataFrame with estimated values filled in.
- This method is advantageous for datasets requiring smooth transitions in numeric values.

5. Count Missing Values

What is Count Missing Values?

Counts the number of missing values in each column.

Syntax:

```
df.isnull().sum()
```

Syntax Explanation:

- Combines isnull() with sum() to count True values (missing values) in each column.
- Useful for assessing the extent of missing data and determining the need for further handling.
- Works efficiently with large datasets, providing quick insights into data quality.
- Helps prioritize columns for detailed treatment or adjustment based on the missing value count.

Example:
```
missing_counts = df.isnull().sum()
print("Missing value counts:\n", missing_counts)
```

Example Explanation:
- Outputs the count of missing values in each column: Name   1
  Age   1
  dtype: int64
- This information helps prioritize columns for missing value treatment.

Real-Life Project:

Project Name: Cleaning Customer Data
Project Goal:
Handle missing data in a customer dataset by filling or removing missing values, ensuring the dataset is ready for analysis.
Code for This Project:
```
import pandas as pd
# Create a DataFrame with customer data
customer_data = {
    'CustomerID': [1, 2, 3, 4],
    'Name': ['Alice', 'Bob', None, 'David'],
    'Age': [25, None, 35, 40],
    'PurchaseAmount': [100, 200, None, 400]
}
df = pd.DataFrame(customer_data)
# Fill missing values
filled_df = df.fillna({
    'Name': 'Unknown',
    'Age': df['Age'].mean(),
    'PurchaseAmount': df['PurchaseAmount'].median()
})
# Drop rows with all missing values
dropped_df = filled_df.dropna(how='all')

print("Cleaned DataFrame:\n", dropped_df)
```

Expanded Features:
- Demonstrates multiple methods to handle missing values.
- Combines filling and dropping strategies for a cleaner dataset.
- Prepares data for further analysis or machine learning.

Expected Output:

Cleaned DataFrame:

```
   CustomerID     Name   Age   PurchaseAmount
0           1    Alice  25.0            100.0
1           2      Bob  33.3            200.0
2           3  Unknown  35.0            300.0
3           4    David  40.0            400.0
```

This project showcases practical techniques for managing missing data, ensuring data quality and readiness for analysis.

Chapter-8 Data Manipulation with Pandas

Data manipulation is at the core of any data analysis process, and Pandas provides a comprehensive toolkit for transforming, reshaping, and analyzing data. This chapter explores key operations such as filtering, grouping, merging, and reshaping DataFrames to prepare datasets for deeper insights and analysis.

Key Characteristics of Data Manipulation with Pandas:

- **Versatility:** Supports a wide range of operations, from simple column transformations to complex group-based aggregations.
- **Integration:** Works seamlessly with NumPy, Matplotlib, and other Python libraries.
- **Efficiency:** Optimized for handling large datasets efficiently.
- **Flexibility:** Offers intuitive and chainable methods for multi-step transformations.
- **Scalability:** Handles both small-scale and large-scale datasets effectively.

Basic Rules for Data Manipulation:

1. Use DataFrame methods like `apply()`, `groupby()`, and `merge()` for versatile operations.
2. Operations on DataFrames are vectorized for performance.
3. The original DataFrame is not modified unless `inplace=True` is specified.
4. Missing data can be handled within manipulation workflows using `fillna()` or `dropna()`.

Best Practices:

- **Plan Transformations:** Outline the required steps before starting to manipulate data.
- **Use Chainable Methods:** Combine multiple operations for concise and readable code.
- **Profile Performance:** Use tools like `df.info()` and `df.memory_usage()` to ensure efficiency.
- **Leverage Documentation:** Pandas has extensive documentation for understanding complex operations.
- **Test on Subsets:** Test transformations on a smaller sample of the

dataset to ensure correctness.

Syntax Table:

SL No	Function/ Feature	Syntax/Example	Description
1	Apply Function	`df['column'].app ly(func)`	Applies a function element-wise.
2	Group By	`df.groupby('colu mn').mean()`	Groups data and computes aggregates.
3	Merge DataFram es	`pd.merge(df1, df2, on='key')`	Combines two DataFrames on a key column.
4	Pivot Table	`df.pivot_table(v alues, index, ...)`	Reshapes data into a pivot table.
5	Sort Values	`df.sort_values(b y='column')`	Sorts the DataFrame by column values.

Syntax Explanation:

1. Apply Function

What is Apply Function?
Applies a function to each element of a Series or DataFrame column, enabling transformations and complex computations on data. This method is versatile and can handle a variety of operations, including applying lambda functions, custom functions, or even integrating with external libraries for advanced processing. It supports row-wise or column-wise transformations in a DataFrame when combined with `axis`.
Syntax:
`df['column'].apply(func)`

Syntax Explanation:
- `df`: The input DataFrame to manipulate.
- `column`: The target column where the function is applied.
- `func`: A custom or built-in function to apply to each element. This

can include mathematical transformations, string operations, or complex logical manipulations.
- When combined with df.apply(), this can be extended to apply functions to entire rows or columns.
- Returns a Series with the transformed values, which can be assigned to a new column.
- Allows flexibility to apply Python or external library functions for advanced transformations.

Example:
```
import pandas as pd
# Create a DataFrame
data = {'Name': ['Alice', 'Bob', 'Charlie'], 'Age':
[25, 30, 35]}
df = pd.DataFrame(data)
# Apply a function to double the age
df['Double_Age'] = df['Age'].apply(lambda x: x * 2)
print(df)
```

Example Explanation:
- Doubles each value in the Age column.
- Outputs:
  ```
        Name   Age   Double_Age
  0    Alice    25          50
  1      Bob    30          60
  2  Charlie    35          70
  ```
- This operation is particularly useful for creating new features or preparing data for machine learning workflows.

2. Group By

What is Group By?
Groups data based on a specified column and applies an aggregate function to summarize or transform the grouped data. This operation is highly flexible, supporting built-in aggregation functions like mean(), sum(), count(), as well as custom user-defined functions. It enables targeted analysis by grouping and aggregating data according to specific categories, making it indispensable for summarizing and analyzing large datasets.

Syntax:
```
df.groupby('column').agg_func()
```
Syntax Explanation:
- groupby('column'): Groups rows by the unique values in the column, creating a GroupBy object.
- agg_func: Built-in aggregation functions like mean(), sum(), min(), max(), or custom aggregation methods.
- Supports multiple aggregations using a dictionary to specify functions for different columns.
- Returns a grouped DataFrame or Series that can be further analyzed or visualized.
- This method enables hierarchical indexing when grouping by multiple columns, allowing for multi-level group analysis.

Example:
```
data = {'Department': ['HR', 'IT', 'HR', 'IT'],
'Salary': [50000, 60000, 45000, 70000]}
df = pd.DataFrame(data)
grouped = df.groupby('Department').mean()
print(grouped)
```
Example Explanation:
- Groups salaries by department and calculates the mean.
- Outputs:
```
                   Salary
Department
HR              47500.0
IT              65000.0
```
- This approach is useful for generating summarized reports or understanding patterns in categorical data.

3. Merge DataFrames

What is Merge DataFrames?

Combines two DataFrames based on a common key column, facilitating the integration of related datasets. This operation supports different types of joins, including inner, outer, left, and right joins, enabling flexible merging strategies to align data according to specific requirements. Merging is crucial for combining data from different sources into a unified structure for analysis.

Syntax:
```
pd.merge(df1, df2, on='key')
```

Syntax Explanation:
- df1 and df2: Input DataFrames to merge.
- on='key': Specifies the column common to both DataFrames used for merging.
- how: Specifies the type of join ('inner', 'outer', 'left', 'right'). Default is 'inner'.
- suffixes: Adds suffixes to overlapping column names for clarity.
- Returns a merged DataFrame with aligned rows and combined columns.

Example:
```
data1 = {'ID': [1, 2], 'Name': ['Alice', 'Bob']}
data2 = {'ID': [1, 2], 'Department': ['HR', 'IT']}
df1 = pd.DataFrame(data1)
df2 = pd.DataFrame(data2)
merged_df = pd.merge(df1, df2, on='ID')
print(merged_df)
```

Example Explanation:
- Merges df1 and df2 on the ID column.
- Outputs: ID   Name Department
  0   1   Alice   HR
  1   2   Bob   IT
- This process enables creating comprehensive datasets by combining attributes from different sources.

4. Pivot Table

What is Pivot Table?
Creates a table where data is aggregated based on specified rows and columns, allowing for detailed analysis and summarization. This operation is essential for organizing data into a structured format, making it easier to identify trends, comparisons, and patterns across categories. Pivot tables are powerful tools for exploratory data analysis and reporting.

Syntax:
```
df.pivot_table(values, index, columns, aggfunc='mean')
```
Syntax Explanation:
- values: Specifies the column to aggregate, such as sales or profit.
- index: Defines the rows in the pivot table.
- columns: Defines the columns in the pivot table.
- aggfunc: The aggregation function applied to values. Default is 'mean', but other functions like sum, count, or custom functions can be used.
- Supports handling missing data through the fill_value parameter.
- Returns a reshaped DataFrame suitable for analysis or visualization.

Example:
```
data = {'City': ['NY', 'LA', 'NY'], 'Product': ['A', 'A', 'B'], 'Sales': [100, 200, 150]}
df = pd.DataFrame(data)
pivot = df.pivot_table(values='Sales', index='City', columns='Product', aggfunc='sum')
print(pivot)
```
Example Explanation:
- Aggregates sales by city and product.
- Outputs:
```
Product      A       B
City
LA        200.0    NaN
NY        100.0   150.0
```
- Enables comparing sales performance across different cities and products.

5. Sort Values

What is Sort Values?
Sorts the DataFrame by column values in ascending or descending order, enabling efficient organization of data for better readability and analysis. This operation is particularly useful for ranking, prioritization, and identifying trends within datasets, especially for large or unordered data.

Syntax:
```
df.sort_values(by='column', ascending=True)
```

Syntax Explanation:
- by='column': Specifies the column to sort by. Multiple columns can be specified as a list.
- ascending: If True, sorts in ascending order; otherwise, sorts in descending order.
- inplace: Modifies the DataFrame in place if set to True. Default is False.
- Returns a sorted DataFrame or modifies the original if inplace=True.
- Allows hierarchical sorting when multiple columns are specified.

Example:
```
data = {'Name': ['Alice', 'Bob'], 'Age': [30, 25]}
df = pd.DataFrame(data)
sorted_df = df.sort_values(by='Age', ascending=True)
print(sorted_df)
```

Example Explanation:
- Sorts the DataFrame by the Age column in ascending order.
- Outputs: Name   Age
  ```
  1    Bob    25
  0    Alice  30
  ```
- This method is essential for ranking or preparing data for visual representation.

Real-Life Project:

Project Name: Sales Analysis

Project Goal:
Analyze sales data to identify top-performing products and regions.

Code for This Project:

```python
import pandas as pd
# Create a sales DataFrame
data = {
    'Region': ['North', 'South', 'North', 'East'],
    'Product': ['A', 'B', 'A', 'B'],
    'Sales': [200, 300, 150, 100]
}
df = pd.DataFrame(data)

# Group by Region and Product
grouped = df.groupby(['Region', 'Product']).sum()

# Sort by Sales
sorted_sales = grouped.sort_values(by='Sales',
ascending=False)

print("Top Performing Regions and Products:\n",
sorted_sales)
```

Expanded Features:
- Demonstrates grouping and sorting for detailed insights.
- Highlights the use of multi-level indices in analysis.
- Supports advanced reporting and decision-making processes.

Expected Output:

Top Performing Regions and Products:

```
                    Sales
Region  Product
South   B            300
North   A            200
North   A            150
East    B            100
```

This project showcases key data manipulation techniques for analyzing and summarizing data effectively.

Chapter-9 Sorting DataFrames and Series in Pandas

Sorting data is a fundamental operation in data analysis that enables better organization, readability, and prioritization of information. Pandas provides powerful and flexible tools for sorting DataFrames and Series by one or more columns, values, or index, both in ascending and descending order. This chapter covers the syntax, examples, and best practices for sorting in Pandas.

Key Characteristics of Sorting in Pandas:

- **Versatility:** Supports sorting by values or index, handling multiple levels of sorting.
- **Customization:** Offers options for sorting order and handling missing values.
- **Performance:** Optimized for large datasets, ensuring efficient sorting.
- **Integration:** Works seamlessly with other Pandas operations like filtering and grouping.

Basic Rules for Sorting:

1. Sorting can be performed on DataFrame columns or Series values.
2. By default, sorting is performed in ascending order.
3. Multiple columns can be sorted simultaneously by specifying a list of column names.
4. Missing values are placed at the end by default.
5. The `inplace` parameter allows for sorting in place, modifying the original data.

Best Practices:

- **Use Sorting for Ranking:** Leverage sorting to rank or prioritize data for analysis.
- **Combine Sorting with Filtering:** Narrow down datasets before sorting for efficiency.
- **Handle Missing Values:** Be mindful of NaNs and specify the `na_position` parameter if needed.
- **Profile Performance:** Use sorting on subsets for large datasets to optimize performance.

Syntax Table:

SL No	Function/Feature	Syntax/Example	Description
1	Sort by Column Values	`df.sort_values(by='column')`	Sorts a DataFrame by one or more columns.
2	Sort by Index	`df.sort_index()`	Sorts a DataFrame or Series by its index.
3	Sort Series by Values	`series.sort_values()`	Sorts a Series by its values.
4	Sort Multi-Index	`df.sort_index(level=0)`	Sorts a DataFrame with a multi-index.
5	Custom Sorting	`df.sort_values(by='column', key=func)`	Sorts using a custom sorting function.

Syntax Explanation:

1. Sort by Column Values

What is Sorting by Column Values?

Sorting by column values arranges the rows of a DataFrame based on the values in one or more columns. This is useful for ranking or organizing data for better readability and analysis.

Syntax:

`df.sort_values(by='column', ascending=True)`

Syntax Explanation:

- `df`: The input DataFrame to be sorted.
- `by='column'`: Specifies the column to sort by. For multiple columns, pass a list.
- `ascending=True`: Sorts in ascending order by default. Set to `False` for descending order.
- `inplace=False`: If True, modifies the original DataFrame.
- `na_position`: Specifies the placement of NaNs, either `'first'` or `'last'` (default).
- Returns a new sorted DataFrame unless `inplace=True` is specified.

Example:

```python
import pandas as pd
# Create a DataFrame
data = {'Name': ['Alice', 'Bob', 'Charlie'], 'Age':
[30, 25, 35]}
df = pd.DataFrame(data)
# Sort by Age
df_sorted = df.sort_values(by='Age', ascending=True)
print(df_sorted)
```

Example Explanation:
- Sorts the DataFrame by the Age column in ascending order.
- Outputs: Name   Age
  - 1   Bob   25
  - 0   Alice   30
  - 2 Charlie   35
- This method is commonly used for ranking and organizing data.

2. Sort by Index

What is Sorting by Index?
Sorting by index arranges the rows or columns of a DataFrame or Series based on their index values.
Syntax:
```python
df.sort_index(axis=0, ascending=True)
```

Syntax Explanation:
- df: The input DataFrame or Series to be sorted.
- axis=0: Sorts rows by default. Use axis=1 to sort columns.
- ascending=True: Sorts in ascending order by default. Set to False for descending order.
- inplace=False: If True, modifies the original data.
- Returns a sorted DataFrame or Series.

Example:

```
data = {'Name': ['Alice', 'Bob'], 'Age': [30, 25]}
df = pd.DataFrame(data, index=['b', 'a'])
sorted_df = df.sort_index()
print(sorted_df)
```

Example Explanation:
- Sorts the DataFrame by its index in ascending order.
- Outputs: Name   Age

  a   Bob   25

  b   Alice   30
- Sorting by index is helpful for aligning data or preparing it for merging.

3. Sort Series by Values

What is Sorting a Series by Values?

Sorting a Series by values arranges its elements in ascending or descending order based on their magnitude or categorical order. This operation is particularly useful for ranking, identifying extremes such as minimum or maximum values, and preparing data for further analysis or visualization.

Syntax:

```
series.sort_values(ascending=True)
```

Syntax Explanation:
- `series`: The Series to be sorted.
- `ascending=True`: Sorts in ascending order by default. Set to `False` for descending order.
- `na_position='last'`: Places NaNs at the end by default. Use `'first'` to place them at the beginning.
- Returns a new sorted Series.

Example:

```
series = pd.Series([3, 1, 2], index=['a', 'b', 'c'])
sorted_series = series.sort_values()
print(sorted_series)
```

Example Explanation:
- Sorts the Series values in ascending order.
- Outputs: b   1

  c   2

  a   3

  ```
  dtype: int64
  ```
- Useful for ranking or identifying minimum/maximum values.

4. Sort Multi-Index

What is Sorting a Multi-Index?
Sorting a multi-index arranges the rows or columns of a DataFrame based on multiple levels of the index.

Syntax:
```
df.sort_index(level=0, ascending=True)
```

Syntax Explanation:
- `df`: The input DataFrame with a multi-index.
- `level=0`: Specifies which index level to sort by.
- `ascending=True`: Sorts in ascending order by default.
- `inplace=False`: If True, modifies the original data.
- Returns a sorted DataFrame.

Example:
```
arrays = [['A', 'A', 'B', 'B'], [1, 2, 1, 2]]
index = pd.MultiIndex.from_arrays(arrays,
names=('Group', 'Number'))
data = [10, 20, 15, 25]
df = pd.DataFrame(data, index=index, columns=['Value'])
sorted_df = df.sort_index(level='Number')
print(sorted_df)
```

Example Explanation:
- Sorts the DataFrame by the Number level of the multi-index.
- Outputs a DataFrame with rows ordered by Number within each Group.

5. Custom Sorting

What is Custom Sorting?
Custom sorting allows applying a user-defined function to determine the order of values in a column.

Syntax:
```
df.sort_values(by='column', key=func)
```

Syntax Explanation:
- df: The input DataFrame to be sorted.
- by='column': Specifies the column to sort by.
- key=func: A function that transforms the column values before sorting.
- Returns a sorted DataFrame.

Example:
```
data = {'Name': ['Alice', 'Bob', 'Charlie'], 'Score':
[88, 95, 85]}
df = pd.DataFrame(data)
sorted_df = df.sort_values(by='Score', key=lambda col:
-col)
print(sorted_df)
```

Example Explanation:
- Applies a custom function to sort Score in descending order.
- Outputs:
  ```
         Name   Score
  1      Bob     95
  0    Alice     88
  2  Charlie     85
  ```

Real-Life Project:

Project Name: Student Performance Analysis

Project Goal:
Rank students based on their performance and identify top performers.

Code for This Project:

```python
import pandas as pd
# Create a student performance DataFrame
data = {
    'Student': ['Alice', 'Bob', 'Charlie'],
    'Math': [90, 80, 85],
    'Science': [85, 95, 80]
}
df = pd.DataFrame(data)

# Compute total scores
df['Total'] = df['Math'] + df['Science']

# Sort by Total Score
ranked_df = df.sort_values(by='Total', ascending=False)

print("Ranked Students:\n", ranked_df)
```

Expanded Features:
- Demonstrates column creation and sorting for ranking.
- Supports identifying high-performing individuals for analysis or rewards.

Expected Output:

Ranked Students:

```
   Student  Math  Science  Total
1      Bob    80       95    175
0    Alice    90       85    175
2  Charlie    85       80    165
```

This project highlights the utility of sorting for evaluating and ranking data effectively.

Chapter-10 Filtering and Querying Data in Pandas

Filtering and querying are essential tools in data analysis, allowing users to isolate specific subsets of data for further analysis. Pandas provides a rich set of methods to filter data using logical conditions, expressions, and query strings. This chapter explores the syntax, examples, and best practices for efficiently filtering and querying data in Pandas.

Key Characteristics of Filtering and Querying in Pandas:

- **Flexibility:** Supports filtering based on multiple conditions and expressions.
- **Integration:** Combines seamlessly with other Pandas operations for complex workflows.
- **Efficiency:** Optimized for handling large datasets and applying logical conditions.
- **Readability:** Offers query strings for intuitive and concise filtering.
- **Versatility:** Enables both row and column-level filtering.

Basic Rules for Filtering and Querying:

1. Logical operators like &, |, and ~ are used for combining conditions.
2. Parentheses are required when combining multiple conditions.
3. The query() method allows string-based filtering.
4. Column names with spaces or special characters require backticks (`) in query strings.
5. Use .loc[] for label-based filtering and .iloc[] for index-based filtering.

Best Practices:

- **Validate Conditions:** Double-check logical conditions to avoid unintended results.
- **Optimize Queries:** Use vectorized operations for efficiency.
- **Chain Operations:** Combine filtering with other operations for concise workflows.
- **Leverage Query Strings:** Use query() for improved readability in complex filters.
- **Handle Missing Values:** Filter out or handle rows with NaN values

to maintain data quality.

Syntax Table:

SL No	Function/ Feature	Syntax/Example	Description
1	Logical Filtering	`df[df['column'] > value]`	Filters rows based on conditions.
2	Multiple Conditions	`df[(cond1) & (cond2)]`	Combines multiple conditions for filtering.
3	Query Method	`df.query('column > value')`	Filters rows using a query string.
4	Index Filtering	`df.loc['label']` or `df.iloc[index]`	Filters rows based on index labels or position.
5	Filtering Columns	`df[['col1', 'col2']]`	Selects specific columns from the DataFrame.

Syntax Explanation:

1. Logical Filtering

What is Logical Filtering?

Logical filtering isolates rows in a DataFrame based on a specified condition applied to one or more columns. It is a powerful way to quickly filter data that meets certain criteria, often used in exploratory data analysis.

Syntax:

`df[df['column'] > value]`

Syntax Explanation:

- **Input DataFrame:** `df` is the dataset being filtered.
- **Condition:** The expression `df['column'] > value` defines the filtering criteria, with other operators like <, >=, <=, ==, and != available.
- **Vectorization:** The operation evaluates the condition for all rows

simultaneously, making it highly efficient.

- **Result:** Returns a new filtered DataFrame that includes rows satisfying the condition, leaving the original data unchanged.
- **Chaining:** This method can be combined with additional operations like sorting, grouping, or column selection for more refined workflows.

Example:
```
import pandas as pd
# Create a DataFrame
data = {'Name': ['Alice', 'Bob', 'Charlie'], 'Age':
[25, 30, 35]}
df = pd.DataFrame(data)
# Filter rows where Age > 30
filtered_df = df[df['Age'] > 30]
print(filtered_df)
```

Example Explanation:
- Filters rows where the Age column has values greater than 30.
- Outputs: Name   Age
       2   Charlie   35
- Logical filtering is essential for isolating subsets of data for focused analysis.

2. Multiple Conditions

What is Filtering with Multiple Conditions?
Combines multiple logical conditions to filter rows that satisfy all or any of the specified criteria. This approach enables users to refine data extraction when multiple rules are applied simultaneously.

Syntax:
```
df[(cond1) & (cond2)]
```

Syntax Explanation:
- **Logical Operators:**
    o &: Logical AND, selecting rows that meet both conditions.
    o |: Logical OR, selecting rows that meet at least one

condition.

- o ~: Logical NOT, excluding rows that satisfy the condition.
- **Parentheses:** Mandatory around individual conditions to ensure correct evaluation order.
- **Vectorized Operations:** Applies conditions to all rows efficiently.
- **Result:** Returns a filtered DataFrame containing rows that meet the combined conditions.

Example:
```
# Filter rows where Age > 25 AND Name is not 'Bob'
filtered_df = df[(df['Age'] > 25) & (df['Name'] !=
'Bob')]
print(filtered_df)
```

Example Explanation:
- Filters rows where Age is greater than 25 and Name is not 'Bob'.
- Outputs: Name   Age
  2   Charlie   35
- Combining conditions enhances flexibility for complex filtering scenarios.

3. Query Method

What is the Query Method?
The query() method allows filtering rows using a string-based expression, providing an intuitive and concise syntax for complex conditions.

Syntax:
```
df.query('column > value')
```
Syntax Explanation:
- **Expression:** A string containing the filter condition, such as 'column > value'.
- **Flexibility:** Supports column names with spaces or special characters enclosed in backticks (`).
- **Output:** Returns a filtered DataFrame.
- **Readability:** Preferred for complex filters where logical operators might reduce clarity.

- **Integration:** Compatible with chained operations for seamless workflows.

Example:
```
# Use query to filter rows where Age > 30
filtered_df = df.query('Age > 30')
print(filtered_df)
```
Example Explanation:
- Filters rows where Age is greater than 30 using a query string.
- Outputs the same result as logical filtering but with enhanced readability.

4. Index Filtering

What is Index Filtering?
Filters rows based on their index labels or position using .loc[] or .iloc[]. This method provides precise control over row selection, making it ideal for targeting specific data points.

Syntax:
```
df.loc['label']
# or
df.iloc[index]
```

Syntax Explanation:
- **loc:** Filters rows by index labels, suitable for labeled DataFrames.
- **iloc:** Filters rows by numerical index positions.
- **Range Selection:** Supports slicing and step-based selection for subsets of data.
- **Output:** Returns a Series or DataFrame, depending on the selection.

Example:
```
# Filter the row at index 1
filtered_row = df.iloc[1]
print(filtered_row)
```
Example Explanation:
- Selects the row at index 1.
- Outputs: Name   Bob

```
Age        30
Name: 1, dtype: object
```

5. Filtering Columns

What is Filtering Columns?
Selects specific columns from a DataFrame, allowing users to focus on relevant variables for analysis.
Syntax:
```
df[['col1', 'col2']]
```

Syntax Explanation:
- **Selection:** A list of column names, e.g., ['col1', 'col2'].
- **Output:** Returns a new DataFrame containing only the selected columns.
- **Combination:** Can be used alongside row filtering for creating highly specific data subsets.

Example:
```
# Select the Name and Age columns
filtered_columns = df[['Name', 'Age']]
print(filtered_columns)
```

Example Explanation:
- Isolates the Name and Age columns.
- Outputs: Name Age
  0 Alice   25
  1   Bob   30
  2 Charlie 35

Real-Life Project:

Project Name: Employee Analysis

Project Goal:
Filter employees based on age and department for targeted insights and

reporting.

Code for This Project:

```python
import pandas as pd
# Create an employee DataFrame
data = {
    'Employee': ['Alice', 'Bob', 'Charlie', 'David'],
    'Age': [25, 30, 35, 40],
    'Department': ['HR', 'IT', 'HR', 'IT']
}
df = pd.DataFrame(data)

# Filter employees in HR older than 30
filtered_employees = df[(df['Department'] == 'HR') &
(df['Age'] > 30)]

print("Filtered Employees:\n", filtered_employees)
```

Expanded Features:
- Combines multiple conditions for precise filtering.
- Highlights logical operators and conditional filtering in action.
- Supports customized reporting and targeted analysis.

Expected Output:

Filtered Employees:

	Employee	Age	Department
2	Charlie	35	HR

This project highlights the practical use of filtering techniques for extracting and analyzing data effectively.

Chapter-11 Aggregations and Grouping in Pandas

Aggregations and grouping are essential techniques in data analysis for summarizing and understanding datasets. Pandas provides a flexible and efficient framework for grouping data based on specific criteria and applying aggregation functions to compute summary statistics. This chapter explores the syntax, examples, and best practices for aggregating and grouping data in Pandas.

Key Characteristics of Aggregations and Grouping

- **Flexibility:** Supports a wide range of aggregation functions, including built-in and custom functions.
- **Scalability:** Efficiently handles large datasets with complex grouping operations.
- **Integration:** Combines seamlessly with other Pandas operations for comprehensive analysis.
- **Customizability:** Allows multi-level grouping and multi-function aggregation.
- **Clarity:** Simplifies exploratory data analysis by providing concise summaries.

Basic Rules for Aggregations and Grouping

1. Use groupby() to specify the column(s) for grouping data.
2. Apply aggregation functions like mean(), sum(), count(), or custom functions.
3. Grouping can be hierarchical, allowing multi-level group structures.
4. Aggregation can involve single or multiple functions.
5. Chaining operations enables further transformations on grouped data.

Best Practices

- **Understand the Data:** Analyze the structure and composition of the dataset before grouping.
- **Use Named Aggregations:** Clearly label aggregated columns for

readability.

- **Combine Aggregations:** Apply multiple aggregation functions to extract more insights.
- **Optimize Performance:** Use vectorized operations for efficiency.
- **Handle Missing Data:** Address missing values before aggregation to avoid misleading results.

Syntax Table

SL No	Function/Feature	Syntax/Example	Description
1	Basic Grouping and Aggregation	`df.groupby('column').mean()`	Groups data by column and computes mean.
2	Multi-Level Grouping	`df.groupby(['col1', 'col2']).sum()`	Groups data by multiple columns.
3	Named Aggregations	`df.groupby('column').agg({'col1': 'mean', 'col2': 'sum'})`	Aggregates data with custom labels.
4	Custom Aggregations	`df.groupby('column').agg(custom_func)`	Applies user-defined aggregation functions.
5	Transformations on Groups	`df.groupby('column').transform('mean')`	Applies transformations and retains the original structure.

Syntax Explanation

1. Basic Grouping and Aggregation

What is Basic Grouping and Aggregation?
Basic grouping and aggregation involve dividing data into groups based on unique values in a column and applying a summary function to each group.

Syntax:
```
df.groupby('column').mean()
```

Syntax Explanation:
- **Input DataFrame:** df is the dataset to be grouped.
- **Grouping Column:** The groupby('column') method creates groups based on unique values in the specified column.
- **Aggregation Function:** Functions like mean(), sum(), or count() summarize the grouped data.
- **Output:** Returns a new DataFrame with the grouping column as the index and aggregated values for other columns.
- **Versatility:** Can be applied to numeric and non-numeric columns with appropriate functions.

Example:
```
import pandas as pd
# Create a DataFrame
data = {'Department': ['HR', 'IT', 'HR', 'IT'],
'Salary': [50000, 60000, 45000, 70000]}
df = pd.DataFrame(data)
# Group by Department and calculate the mean Salary
grouped = df.groupby('Department').mean()
print(grouped)
```

Example Explanation:
- Groups salaries by Department and calculates the mean.
- Outputs: Salary
  Department
  HR   47500.0
  IT   65000.0

2. Multi-Level Grouping

What is Multi-Level Grouping?
Multi-level grouping divides data based on unique combinations of values

in multiple columns, allowing for hierarchical analysis.

Syntax:
```
df.groupby(['col1', 'col2']).sum()
```

Syntax Explanation:
- **Grouping Columns:** Lists multiple columns for grouping, creating a hierarchical index.
- **Aggregation Function:** Summarizes grouped data using functions like sum(), count(), or custom methods.
- **Output:** Returns a DataFrame with a multi-level index and aggregated values for remaining columns.
- **Customization:** Allows specifying different aggregation functions for each column.

Example:
```
# Group by Department and Job Title, then calculate
total Salary
data = {
    'Department': ['HR', 'HR', 'IT', 'IT'],
    'Job Title': ['Manager', 'Analyst', 'Manager',
'Analyst'],
    'Salary': [60000, 50000, 80000, 70000]
}
df = pd.DataFrame(data)
grouped = df.groupby(['Department', 'Job Title']).sum()
print(grouped)
```

Example Explanation:
- Groups salaries by Department and Job Title.
- Outputs:

```
                           Salary
Department Job Title
HR         Analyst         50000
           Manager         60000
IT         Analyst         70000
           Manager         80000
```

3. Named Aggregations

What are Named Aggregations?
Named aggregations assign custom labels to aggregated columns, improving clarity and readability of the results.
Syntax:
```
df.groupby('column').agg({'col1': 'mean', 'col2': 'sum'})
```

Syntax Explanation:
- **Dictionary Input:** The agg() method accepts a dictionary where keys are column names and values are aggregation functions.
- **Customization:** Allows specifying different aggregation functions for different columns.
- **Output:** Returns a DataFrame with renamed columns based on the specified aggregations.
- **Clarity:** Enhances interpretability by explicitly naming aggregated results.

Example:
```
# Aggregate mean Salary and sum Bonus by Department
data = {
    'Department': ['HR', 'IT', 'HR', 'IT'],
    'Salary': [50000, 60000, 45000, 70000],
    'Bonus': [5000, 7000, 4000, 8000]
}
df = pd.DataFrame(data)
aggs = df.groupby('Department').agg({'Salary': 'mean', 'Bonus': 'sum'})
print(aggs)
```

Example Explanation:
- Aggregates mean Salary and total Bonus for each Department.
- Outputs:

```
                Salary   Bonus
Department
HR              47500    9000
IT              65000    15000
```

4. Custom Aggregations

What are Custom Aggregations?
Custom aggregations use user-defined functions to summarize grouped data in non-standard ways.
Syntax:
```
df.groupby('column').agg(custom_func)
```

Syntax Explanation:
- **Custom Function:** A Python function or lambda expression defining the aggregation logic.
- **Application:** Applied to each group separately.
- **Output:** Returns aggregated values based on the custom function.
Example:
```
# Calculate the range of Salary for each Department
def salary_range(group):
    return group.max() - group.min()

salary_range_by_dept =
df.groupby('Department')['Salary'].agg(salary_range)
print(salary_range_by_dept)
```

Example Explanation:
- Calculates the range of Salary for each Department using a custom function.
- Outputs the difference between maximum and minimum salaries.

5. Transformations on Groups

What are Transformations on Groups?
Transformations apply functions to group values and return a DataFrame of the same shape, enabling direct comparisons with the original data.
Syntax:
```
df.groupby('column').transform('mean')
```

Syntax Explanation:

- **Transform Function:** Computes group-wise statistics while retaining the original DataFrame structure.
- **Applications:** Useful for normalization, scaling, or adding derived columns.
- **Output:** Returns a transformed DataFrame with the same shape as the input.

Example:

```
# Add a column with mean Salary per Department
df['Mean_Salary'] =
df.groupby('Department')['Salary'].transform('mean')
print(df)
```

Example Explanation:

- Adds a column Mean_Salary showing the average salary for each Department.
- Retains the original structure of the DataFrame while adding contextual insights.

Real-Life Project

Project Name: Employee Salary Analysis
Project Goal

The objective is to analyze salary distributions and departmental bonuses to uncover patterns, trends, and potential outliers. This project demonstrates the use of grouping and aggregation techniques to extract meaningful insights from the data.

Code for This Project

```
import pandas as pd
# Create an employee DataFrame
data = {
    'Employee': ['Alice', 'Bob', 'Charlie', 'David'],
    'Department': ['HR', 'IT', 'HR', 'IT'],
    'Salary': [50000, 60000, 45000, 70000],
    'Bonus': [5000, 7000, 4000, 8000]
}
df = pd.DataFrame(data)
```

```python
# Group by Department and compute aggregations
aggregated = df.groupby('Department').agg({
    'Salary': ['mean', 'max', 'min'],
    'Bonus': 'sum'
})

print("Aggregated Data:\n", aggregated)
```

Expected Output

```
            Salary                      Bonus
            mean      max     min       sum
Department
HR          47500.0 50000   45000   9000
IT          65000.0 70000   60000 15000
```

Part 3: Data Cleaning and Transformation

Chapter-12 Handling Duplicate Data in Pandas

Duplicate data can skew analysis and lead to incorrect insights, making it essential to identify and handle duplicates effectively. Pandas offers intuitive and powerful tools to detect, remove, and manage duplicate rows and columns. This chapter provides detailed insights into the methods and best practices for handling duplicate data in Pandas.

Key Characteristics of Handling Duplicate Data in Pandas:

- **Detection:** Identify duplicate rows or columns based on specific criteria.
- **Flexibility:** Options to define duplication based on entire rows, specific columns, or subsets.
- **Efficiency:** Optimized for large datasets, ensuring quick operations.
- **Customization:** Configure methods to retain, remove, or flag duplicates as per requirements.
- **Integration:** Combines seamlessly with other Pandas functions for advanced workflows.

Basic Rules for Handling Duplicates:

1. Use `duplicated()` to identify duplicate rows.
2. The `drop_duplicates()` method removes duplicate rows while keeping the first or last occurrence.
3. Duplicates can be flagged based on all columns or a subset.
4. Customizable behavior allows retaining specific rows with parameters like `keep='first'` or `keep=False`.
5. Ensure proper indexing for efficient duplicate handling.

Best Practices:

- **Assess Duplicates First:** Use `duplicated()` to identify duplicates before removal.
- **Use Subsets:** Limit duplicate checks to relevant columns to avoid unnecessary operations.
- **Validate Data Integrity:** Ensure no essential information is lost

when removing duplicates.

- **Combine with Filters:** Integrate duplicate handling with data cleaning workflows.
- **Profile Performance:** Use Pandas profiling tools to handle duplicates efficiently in large datasets.

Syntax Table:

SL No	Function/Fe ature	Syntax/Example	Description
1	Identify Duplicates	df.duplicated()	Flags duplicate rows in the DataFrame.
2	Drop Duplicates	df.drop_duplicat es()	Removes duplicate rows based on criteria.
3	Subset for Duplicates	df.duplicated(su bset=['col1', 'col2'])	Identifies duplicates based on specific columns.
4	Keep Parameter	df.drop_duplicat es(keep='last')	Retains the last occurrence of duplicates.
5	Column-Wise Duplicates	df.T.duplicated( )	Identifies duplicate columns in a DataFrame.

Syntax Explanation:

1. Identify Duplicates

What is Identifying Duplicates?
Identifies rows in a DataFrame that are exact duplicates of earlier rows. Duplicate rows are flagged for inspection, enabling targeted cleaning of redundant data.

Syntax:
df.duplicated()

Syntax Explanation:

- **Input DataFrame:** df is the DataFrame where duplicates are to be identified.

- **Default Behavior:** Compares all columns in the DataFrame to detect duplicates.
- **Output:** Returns a Boolean Series with True for duplicate rows and False for unique rows.
- **Custom Subsets:** Use the subset parameter to limit the comparison to specific columns.
- **Keep Parameter:** Determines which occurrence of a duplicate to consider as unique:
  - 'first' (default): Marks subsequent occurrences as duplicates.
  - 'last': Marks earlier occurrences as duplicates.
  - False: Marks all occurrences of duplicates as True.

Example:
```
import pandas as pd
# Create a DataFrame
data = {'Name': ['Alice', 'Bob', 'Alice'], 'Age': [25, 30, 25]}
df = pd.DataFrame(data)
# Identify duplicates
duplicates = df.duplicated()
print(duplicates)
```

Example Explanation:
- Flags duplicate rows (by default, starting from the second occurrence): 0   False
  ```
  1      False
  2      True
  dtype: bool
  ```

- This allows you to inspect which rows are redundant for cleaning or removal.

2. Drop Duplicates

What is Dropping Duplicates?
Removes duplicate rows from a DataFrame while keeping one occurrence (default is the first occurrence). This method is essential for creating clean and concise datasets.

Syntax:
```
df.drop_duplicates(keep='first')
```

Syntax Explanation:
- **Input DataFrame:** df is the DataFrame to clean.
- **Keep Parameter:**
  - `'first'` (default): Retains the first occurrence of duplicates.
  - `'last'`: Retains the last occurrence.
  - `False`: Removes all occurrences of duplicates.
- **Subset Parameter:**
  - Specify columns to consider when identifying duplicates using `subset=['col1', 'col2']`.
- **Inplace:** If True, modifies the original DataFrame; otherwise, returns a new DataFrame.
- **Performance:** Efficiently removes duplicates in large datasets by leveraging vectorized operations.

Example:
```
# Drop duplicate rows while keeping the first
occurrence
cleaned_df = df.drop_duplicates()
print(cleaned_df)
```

Example Explanation:
- Removes duplicate rows, retaining the first occurrence:
  ```
  Name   Age
  0   Alice    25
  1    Bob     30
  ```

- Ensures that redundant data does not skew analyses or reports.

3. Subset for Duplicates

What is Subset-Based Duplicate Identification?
Identifies duplicates based on specific columns rather than the entire row. This method is particularly useful when some columns are not relevant for duplication checks.

Syntax:
```
df.duplicated(subset=['col1', 'col2'])
```

Syntax Explanation:
- **Subset Parameter:** Defines the list of columns to include in the duplicate comparison.
- **Default Behavior:** If no subset is specified, all columns are considered.
- **Output:** A Boolean Series indicating duplicate rows based on the subset.
- **Chaining:** Combine with filtering to isolate specific duplicates for further inspection or removal.

Example:
```
# Identify duplicates based on the 'Name' column
duplicates = df.duplicated(subset=['Name'])
print(duplicates)
```

Example Explanation:
- Flags duplicate rows based only on the Name column: 0 False
  ```
  1    False
  2    True
  dtype: bool
  ```

- This allows focusing on specific aspects of duplication.

4. Keep Parameter

What is the Keep Parameter?
Controls which occurrence of duplicate rows to retain when dropping duplicates. This flexibility is crucial for retaining data based on specific requirements.

Syntax:
```
df.drop_duplicates(keep='last')
```

Syntax Explanation:
- **Keep Parameter:**
  - 'first': Retains the first occurrence and removes

subsequent duplicates.
- o 'last': Retains the last occurrence and removes earlier duplicates.
- o False: Removes all occurrences of duplicates.
- **Behavior:** Applies the specified retention logic to all or a subset of columns.
- **Result:** Returns a DataFrame with duplicates removed as per the specified logic.

Example:

```
# Drop duplicates while keeping the last occurrence
cleaned_df = df.drop_duplicates(keep='last')
print(cleaned_df)
```

Example Explanation:
- Removes duplicates but retains the last occurrence:
  ```
  Name   Age
  1    Bob    30
  2    Alice  25
  ```

- This method ensures the most recent or relevant data is preserved.

5. Column-Wise Duplicates

What is Column-Wise Duplicate Detection?
Detects duplicate columns by transposing the DataFrame and using duplicated(). This is helpful for identifying redundant columns in datasets.

Syntax:

```
df.T.duplicated()
```

Syntax Explanation:
- **Transpose:** Converts columns to rows using df.T, enabling column-wise analysis.
- **Duplicated:** Identifies duplicate columns in the transposed DataFrame.
- **Output:** A Boolean Series indicating which columns are duplicates.
- **Usage:** Ideal for removing redundant columns and optimizing

dataset structure.

Example:
```
# Detect duplicate columns
data = {'A': [1, 2, 3], 'B': [1, 2, 3], 'C': [4, 5, 6]}
df = pd.DataFrame(data)
duplicates = df.T.duplicated()
print(duplicates)
```

Example Explanation:
- Flags duplicate columns: A   False
  B   True
  C   False
  dtype: bool
- Allows users to clean up redundant columns efficiently.

Real-Life Project:

Project Name: Customer Data Cleanup

Project Goal:

Identify and remove duplicate customer records to ensure accurate reporting and analysis.

Code for This Project:
```
import pandas as pd
# Create a customer DataFrame
data = {
    'CustomerID': [1, 2, 3, 1],
    'Name': ['Alice', 'Bob', 'Charlie', 'Alice'],
    'Purchase': [100, 200, 300, 100]
}
df = pd.DataFrame(data)

# Identify duplicates
duplicates = df.duplicated(subset=['CustomerID',
'Name'])
print("Duplicate Flags:\n", duplicates)

# Drop duplicates
cleaned_df = df.drop_duplicates(subset=['CustomerID',
'Name'])
```

```
print("Cleaned DataFrame:\n", cleaned_df)
```

Expected Output:

Duplicate Flags:

```
0      False
1      False
2      False
3       True
dtype: bool
```

Cleaned DataFrame:

	CustomerID	Name	Purchase
0	1	Alice	100
1	2	Bob	200
2	3	Charlie	300

This project demonstrates the practical application of duplicate handling techniques to maintain data integrity and accuracy in customer datasets.

Chapter-13 Applying Functions with apply and map in Pandas

Applying functions is a cornerstone of data transformation and analysis. Pandas provides the apply and map methods for applying functions to Series or DataFrames, offering unparalleled flexibility and efficiency for data manipulation. This chapter explores their usage, syntax, and practical applications.

Key Characteristics of apply and map in Pandas:

- **Versatility:** Apply custom or built-in functions to transform data.
- **Efficiency:** Optimized for vectorized operations on large datasets.
- **Flexibility:** Works with row-wise, column-wise, and element-wise transformations.
- **Integration:** Combines seamlessly with other Pandas functions for advanced workflows.
- **Ease of Use:** Intuitive methods for applying functions with minimal code.

Basic Rules for apply and map:

1. Use apply for row-wise or column-wise transformations in DataFrames.
2. Use map for element-wise transformations in Series.
3. Functions can be built-in, user-defined, or lambda expressions.
4. The result depends on the return type of the applied function.
5. Ensure functions are compatible with the structure of the DataFrame or Series.

Best Practices:

- **Optimize Functions:** Use vectorized operations where possible for better performance.
- **Validate Outputs:** Check the results of the applied function to ensure correctness.
- **Handle Missing Data:** Use functions that account for NaN values to avoid errors.
- **Leverage Lambda Functions:** Use concise lambda expressions for simple transformations.
- **Test on Subsets:** Apply functions on small subsets before scaling

to larger datasets.

Syntax Table:

SL No	Method	Syntax/Example	Description
1	apply	`df.apply(func, axis=0)`	Applies a function along an axis of a DataFrame.
2	applymap	`df.applymap(func)`	Applies a function element-wise across a DataFrame.
3	map	`series.map(func)`	Applies a function element-wise to a Series.
4	Lambda Functions	`df['col'].apply(lambda x: x*2)`	Uses anonymous functions for transformations.
5	Conditional Logic	`series.map(lambda x: x if x > 0 else 0)`	Applies conditional logic to Series elements.

Syntax Explanation:

1. Using apply

What is apply?
The apply method allows users to apply a function along the rows or columns of a DataFrame. It is versatile for row-wise or column-wise operations.
Syntax:
`df.apply(func, axis=0)`

Syntax Explanation:
- **df:** The DataFrame on which the function will be applied.
- **func:** The function to apply. This can be a built-in function, user-defined function, or lambda expression.
- **axis:** Determines the direction of application:
    - `axis=0`: Applies the function column-wise (default).
    - `axis=1`: Applies the function row-wise.

- **Returns:** A Series or DataFrame, depending on the function output.

Example:
```
import pandas as pd
# Create a DataFrame
data = {'A': [1, 2, 3], 'B': [4, 5, 6]}
df = pd.DataFrame(data)
# Apply a function column-wise
df_sum = df.apply(sum, axis=0)
print(df_sum)
```

Example Explanation:
- Applies the sum function to each column of the DataFrame.
- Outputs a Series with the column-wise sum: A   6
  B   15
  dtype: int64

- This method is ideal for aggregation and summary statistics.

2. Using `applymap`

What is applymap?
The `applymap` method applies a function element-wise to every entry in a DataFrame. It is specifically designed for element-wise transformations.

Syntax:
```
df.applymap(func)
```

Syntax Explanation:
- **df:** The DataFrame to transform.
- **func:** A function to apply to each element. This can be a built-in or user-defined function.
- **Returns:** A new DataFrame with the transformed values.
- **Use Case:** Ideal for element-wise transformations like formatting or scaling values.

Example:
```
# Square each element in the DataFrame
df_squared = df.applymap(lambda x: x**2)
```

```
print(df_squared)
```

Example Explanation:
- Squares each element in the DataFrame: A   B
  0   1   16
  1   4   25
  2   9   36

- Useful for element-wise mathematical or text transformations.

3. Using map

What is map?

The map method applies a function element-wise to a Series. It is efficient for applying simple or complex transformations to Series data.

Syntax:

```
series.map(func)
```

Syntax Explanation:
- **series:** The Series to transform.
- **func:** The function to apply. This can be a built-in function, user-defined function, dictionary for mapping values, or a Series.
- **Returns:** A transformed Series with the applied function.
- **Versatility:** Supports conditional logic and value replacements.

Example:

```
# Map a function to double each value
doubled = df['A'].map(lambda x: x * 2)
print(doubled)
```

Example Explanation:
- Doubles each value in column A: 0   2
  1   4
  2   6
  Name: A, dtype: int64

- Efficient for applying transformations to Series data.

4. Lambda Functions

What are Lambda Functions?
Lambda functions are anonymous functions defined using the `lambda` keyword. They are commonly used for short, single-expression transformations.

Syntax:
```
df['col'].apply(lambda x: x * 2)
```

Syntax Explanation:
- **lambda x: x * 2:** A lambda function that doubles the input.
- **Integration:** Can be used with `apply`, `map`, or other Pandas methods.
- **Returns:** A Series or DataFrame with the transformed values.
- **Best Use:** Ideal for concise, one-line operations.

Example:
```
# Triple the values in column A
tripled = df['A'].apply(lambda x: x * 3)
print(tripled)
```

Example Explanation:
- Triples each value in column A: 0   3
  ```
  1      6
  2      9
  Name: A, dtype: int64
  ```

5. Conditional Logic

What is Conditional Logic?
Applies conditions to data and assigns values based on the conditions. This is particularly useful for feature engineering and data cleaning.

Syntax:
```
series.map(lambda x: x if x > 0 else 0)
```

Syntax Explanation:
- **Condition:** Specifies the logic to apply to each element.
- **Returns:** A Series with the conditionally transformed values.

- **Flexibility:** Enables creation of new features based on complex conditions.

Example:
```
# Replace negative values with 0
non_negative = df['A'].map(lambda x: x if x > 0 else 0)
print(non_negative)
```

Example Explanation:
- Replaces negative values in column A with 0: 0   1
    1   2
    2   3
    Name: A, dtype: int64

Real-Life Project:

Project Name: Data Normalization

Project Goal:

Apply transformations to normalize and scale data for machine learning.

Code for This Project:
```
import pandas as pd
# Create a DataFrame with raw data
data = {
    'Feature1': [10, 20, 30],
    'Feature2': [5, 15, 25]
}
df = pd.DataFrame(data)

# Normalize each feature
def normalize(x):
    return (x - x.min()) / (x.max() - x.min())

normalized_df = df.apply(normalize, axis=0)
print("Normalized DataFrame:\n", normalized_df)
```
Expected Output:
```
Normalized DataFrame:
   Feature1  Feature2
0       0.0       0.0
1       0.5       0.5
2       1.0       1.0
```

Chapter-14 String Manipulation in Pandas

String manipulation is a vital part of data preprocessing and cleaning, especially when dealing with textual data. Pandas provides a robust set of tools for string operations through its `.str` accessor, enabling efficient and intuitive transformations. This chapter explores various methods and best practices for manipulating strings in Pandas.

Key Characteristics of String Manipulation in Pandas:
- **Versatility:** Supports operations like splitting, replacing, case conversion, and pattern matching.
- **Integration:** Works seamlessly with other Pandas methods for complex transformations.
- **Efficiency:** Optimized for handling large datasets with textual data.
- **Flexibility:** Allows the use of both Python string methods and regular expressions.
- **Ease of Use:** Intuitive syntax for applying operations to entire Series.

Basic Rules for String Manipulation:
1. Use the `.str` accessor to apply string methods to Pandas Series.
2. Methods are vectorized, applying the operation to all elements in the Series.
3. Many operations support regular expressions for advanced pattern matching.
4. Non-string values are ignored or handled gracefully when using `.str`.
5. Results are returned as a new Series unless specified otherwise.

Best Practices:
- **Clean Data Early:** Perform string operations during the initial data cleaning stages.
- **Avoid Manual Loops:** Use vectorized string methods for better performance.
- **Validate Data Types:** Ensure the Series contains strings to avoid

unexpected results.

- **Use Regular Expressions Judiciously:** Test patterns thoroughly to avoid errors.
- **Chain Operations:** Combine multiple string methods for concise transformations.

Syntax Table:

SL No	Method/Feature	Syntax/Example	Description
1	Case Conversion	df['col'].str.upper()	Converts strings to uppercase.
2	Splitting Strings	df['col'].str.split(delimiter)	Splits strings based on a delimiter.
3	Substring Extraction	df['col'].str.slice(start, stop)	Extracts a substring from each string.
4	Replace Substrings	df['col'].str.replace(pattern, repl)	Replaces occurrences of a pattern or substring.
5	Pattern Matching	df['col'].str.contains(pattern)	Checks if strings contain a specified pattern.

Syntax Explanation:

1. Case Conversion

What is Case Conversion?
Case conversion changes the case of strings in a Series to uppercase, lowercase, or title case.
Syntax:
df['col'].str.upper()

Syntax Explanation:
- **.str:** Accessor to apply string methods to a Pandas Series.
- **upper():** Converts all characters in the string to uppercase.
- **lower() and title():** Methods for lowercase and title case

conversions, respectively.

- **Output:** Returns a Series with converted string values.

Example:
```
import pandas as pd
# Create a DataFrame
data = {'Name': ['Alice', 'Bob', 'Charlie']}
df = pd.DataFrame(data)
# Convert names to uppercase
df['Name_Upper'] = df['Name'].str.upper()
print(df)
```

Example Explanation:

- Converts names to uppercase:

```
      Name  Name_Upper
0    Alice       ALICE
1      Bob         BOB
2  Charlie     CHARLIE
```

- Useful for standardizing text in datasets.

2. Splitting Strings

What is Splitting Strings?
Splitting strings divides each string into a list of substrings based on a specified delimiter.

Syntax:
```
df['col'].str.split(delimiter)
```

Syntax Explanation:

- **delimiter:** The character or pattern used to split the string.
- **Output:** Returns a Series of lists containing the substrings.
- **Expand Parameter:** Use expand=True to split strings into separate columns in a DataFrame.

Example:
```
# Split names based on spaces
df['Name_Split'] = df['Name'].str.split(' ')
print(df)
```

Example Explanation:
- Splits names into a list of words:

Name	Name_Split
0 Alice	[Alice]
1 Bob	[Bob]
2 Charlie	[Charlie]

- Helpful for parsing or tokenizing text data.

3. Substring Extraction

What is Substring Extraction?
Extracts a specific portion of each string based on start and stop indices.
Syntax:
```
df['col'].str.slice(start, stop)
```

Syntax Explanation:
- **start:** The starting index for the substring (inclusive).
- **stop:** The ending index for the substring (exclusive).
- **Output:** Returns a Series with the extracted substrings.

Example:
```
# Extract the first three characters
df['Name_Slice'] = df['Name'].str.slice(0, 3)
print(df)
```

Example Explanation:
- Extracts the first three characters of each name:

Name	Name_Slice
0 Alice	Ali
1 Bob	Bob
2 Charlie	Cha

- Useful for truncating or standardizing text data.

4. Replace Substrings

What is Replacing Substrings?
Replaces all occurrences of a pattern or substring in each string with a specified replacement.

Syntax:

```
df['col'].str.replace(pattern, repl, regex=True)
```

Syntax Explanation:
- **pattern:** The substring or regular expression to replace.
- **repl:** The replacement string.
- **regex:** If True, interprets pattern as a regular expression.
- **Output:** Returns a Series with replaced values.

Example:

```
# Replace 'e' with 'E' in names
df['Name_Replaced'] = df['Name'].str.replace('e', 'E')
print(df)
```

Example Explanation:
- Replaces occurrences of 'e' with 'E':   Name Name_Replaced
  ```
  0   Alice          AlicE
  1     Bob            Bob
  2 Charlie        CharliE
  ```
- Ideal for cleaning or standardizing text.

5. Pattern Matching

What is Pattern Matching?
Checks if strings contain a specific pattern, returning a Boolean Series.

Syntax:

```
df['col'].str.contains(pattern, regex=True)
```

Syntax Explanation:
- **pattern:** The substring or regular expression to search for.
- **regex:** If True, interprets pattern as a regular expression.
- **Output:** Returns a Boolean Series indicating the presence of the pattern.

Example:

```
# Check if names contain the letter 'o'
df['Contains_O'] = df['Name'].str.contains('o')
print(df)
```

Example Explanation:

- Flags names containing 'o':   Name   Contains_O

  ```
  0   Alice          False
  1     Bob           True
  2 Charlie          False
  ```

- Useful for filtering or flagging rows based on text patterns.

Real-Life Project:

Project Name: Email Domain Extraction

Project Goal:
Extract and analyze email domains from a dataset of email addresses.

Code for This Project:

```python
import pandas as pd
# Create a DataFrame with email addresses
data = {'Email': ['alice@example.com', 'bob@test.com',
'charlie@work.org']}
df = pd.DataFrame(data)

# Extract domains from email addresses
df['Domain'] = df['Email'].str.split('@').str[1]
print("Extracted Domains:\n", df)
```

Expected Output:

Extracted Domains:

```
               Email           Domain
0   alice@example.com     example.com
1       bob@test.com        test.com
2   charlie@work.org        work.org
```

This project demonstrates how to use string methods for extracting meaningful information from textual data efficiently.

Chapter-15 Date and Time Operations in Pandas

Handling date and time data is crucial for many data analysis tasks, such as time series analysis, scheduling, and trend analysis. Pandas provides extensive support for working with dates and times, enabling seamless conversion, manipulation, and analysis. This chapter covers essential techniques and best practices for working with date and time data in Pandas.

Key Characteristics of Date and Time Operations in Pandas:

- **Versatility:** Supports a wide range of date and time formats.
- **Integration:** Combines with other Pandas functions for powerful data manipulation.
- **Efficiency:** Optimized for large datasets with temporal data.
- **Flexibility:** Allows operations like resampling, shifting, and rolling window calculations.
- **Ease of Use:** Provides intuitive methods for common date and time transformations.

Basic Rules for Date and Time Operations:

1. Use `pd.to_datetime()` to convert strings or numeric data into datetime objects.
2. Access datetime properties using the `.dt` accessor for Series.
3. Perform arithmetic and comparisons directly on datetime objects.
4. Handle time zones using the `tz` parameter and `.tz_convert()` method.
5. Use date-specific indices for time series data to enable advanced analysis.

Best Practices:

- **Standardize Formats:** Convert all date and time data to a consistent format during preprocessing.
- **Validate Data:** Use error handling to manage invalid date formats.
- **Optimize Storage:** Convert datetime objects to `datetime64` for efficient storage and computation.
- **Use Indexing:** Set datetime columns as the index for time series analysis.

- **Explore Aggregations:** Utilize resampling and grouping for temporal aggregation.

Syntax Table:

SL No	Function/Feature	Syntax/Example	Description
1	Convert to Datetime	`pd.to_datetime(data)`	Converts data to datetime objects.
2	Access Date Properties	`df['col'].dt.year`	Accesses year, month, day, etc., from datetime.
3	Time Zone Handling	`df['col'].dt.tz_convert('UTC')`	Converts datetime to a specific time zone.
4	Date Arithmetic	`df['date1'] - df['date2']`	Performs arithmetic between datetime objects.
5	Resampling	`df.resample('M').mean()`	Aggregates data by a specified time frequency.

Syntax Explanation:

1. Convert to Datetime

What is `pd.to_datetime()`?

Converts data into datetime objects, simplifying time-based calculations and enabling advanced time series analysis, such as resampling, filtering, and trend identification.

Syntax:
`pd.to_datetime(data, format=None, errors='raise')`

Syntax Explanation:
- **data:** The input data (e.g., Series, list, or DataFrame column) to convert.
- **format:** Optional string specifying the datetime format (e.g., `"%Y-%m-%d"`).
- **errors:** Specifies error handling:

- o   `'raise'`: Raises an exception for invalid formats.
  - o   `'coerce'`: Converts invalid formats to NaT (Not a Time).
  - o   `'ignore'`: Returns the input without raising an error.
- **Output:** Returns a Series or DataFrame with datetime objects.

Example:
```
import pandas as pd
# Convert strings to datetime objects
data = ['2023-01-01', '2023-01-02', 'Invalid']
dates = pd.to_datetime(data, errors='coerce')
print(dates)
```

Example Explanation:
- Converts valid strings to datetime objects and invalid entries to NaT: 0   2023-01-01
  1   2023-01-02
  2   NaT
  dtype: datetime64[ns]

2. Access Date Properties

What are Date Properties?
Provides access to specific components of datetime objects, such as year, month, day, and more.

Syntax:
```
df['col'].dt.component
```

Syntax Explanation:
- **.dt:** Accessor for datetime properties in a Series.
- **component:** Property to extract (e.g., year, month, day, hour).
- **Output:** Returns a Series with the extracted property values.

Example:
```
# Extract year and month from a datetime Series
df = pd.DataFrame({'dates': pd.to_datetime(['2023-01-
01', '2023-02-15'])})
df['year'] = df['dates'].dt.year
df['month'] = df['dates'].dt.month
print(df)
```

Example Explanation:
- Extracts the year and month:
  ```
  dates   year    month
  0 2023-01-01   2023        1
  1 2023-02-15   2023        2
  ```

3. Time Zone Handling

What is Time Zone Handling?
Handles time zone conversions and ensures consistency across datetime objects.

Syntax:
```
df['col'].dt.tz_convert(tz)
```

Syntax Explanation:
- **tz:** Specifies the target time zone (e.g., `'UTC'`, `'US/Eastern'`).
- **.dt.tz_localize():** Sets a time zone for naive datetime objects.
- **.dt.tz_convert():** Converts datetime objects to a different time zone.
- **Output:** Returns a Series with adjusted datetime values.

Example:
```
# Convert to UTC time zone
df['dates_utc'] = df['dates'].dt.tz_localize('UTC')
print(df)
```

Example Explanation:
- Adds a UTC time zone to naive datetime objects.

4. Date Arithmetic

What is Date Arithmetic?
Performs operations like addition, subtraction, and comparison on datetime objects.

Syntax:
```
df['date1'] - df['date2']
```

Syntax Explanation:
- **Operands:** Datetime columns or datetime objects.
- **Operation:** Returns a `Timedelta` object for subtraction or a modified datetime object for addition.
- **Output:** A Series of `Timedelta` objects or datetime objects, depending on the operation.

Example:
```
# Calculate the difference between two dates
df['difference'] = pd.to_datetime('2023-02-01') -
df['dates']
print(df)
```

Example Explanation:
- Calculates the difference in days: dates   difference
  ```
  0 2023-01-01     31 days
  1 2023-02-15     -14 days
  ```

5. Resampling

What is Resampling?
Aggregates data at a specified time frequency, such as monthly or weekly.

Syntax:
```
df.resample('frequency').agg_func()
```

Syntax Explanation:
- **frequency:** The resampling frequency (e.g., 'M' for monthly, 'W' for weekly).
- **agg_func:** Aggregation function to apply (e.g., mean, sum, count).
- **Output:** A resampled DataFrame or Series.

Example:
```
# Resample data to monthly frequency
data = {'dates': pd.date_range('2023-01-01', periods=6,
freq='D'), 'value': [10, 20, 30, 40, 50, 60]}
df = pd.DataFrame(data)
df.set_index('dates', inplace=True)
monthly_avg = df.resample('M').mean()
print(monthly_avg)
```

Example Explanation:

- Aggregates daily data into monthly averages:
  ```
  dates value
  2023-01-31    30.0
  ```

Real-Life Project:

Project Name: Sales Trend Analysis
Project Goal:
Analyze sales trends over time, identify peak periods, and calculate month-over-month growth.
Code for This Project:

```python
import pandas as pd
# Create a sales DataFrame
data = {
    'dates': pd.date_range('2023-01-01', periods=60,
freq='D'),
    'sales': [x * 1.05**(i % 30) for i, x in
enumerate(range(60))]
}
df = pd.DataFrame(data)
df.set_index('dates', inplace=True)

# Calculate monthly total sales
monthly_sales = df.resample('M').sum()
print("Monthly Sales:\n", monthly_sales)

# Calculate month-over-month growth
monthly_sales['growth'] =
monthly_sales['sales'].pct_change() * 100
print("Monthly Growth:\n", monthly_sales)
```

Expected Output:
Monthly Sales:

Chapter-16 Merging, Joining, and Concatenating DataFrames in Pandas

Combining datasets is a vital step in data analysis, allowing you to consolidate and enrich your data for comprehensive insights. Pandas provides robust tools for merging, joining, and concatenating DataFrames, supporting a variety of use cases from simple appending to complex relational operations. This chapter covers the key methods, syntax, and practical applications for combining DataFrames effectively.

Key Characteristics of Combining DataFrames:

- **Versatility:** Supports various operations such as merging, joining, and concatenating.
- **Scalability:** Handles small to large datasets efficiently.
- **Flexibility:** Offers multiple join types (inner, outer, left, right) and axis-based concatenation.
- **Integration:** Works seamlessly with other Pandas operations for further data manipulation.

Basic Rules for Combining DataFrames:

1. For merging, both DataFrames must share a common key column or index.
2. Joining is designed for combining DataFrames on their indices.
3. Concatenation stacks DataFrames either vertically or horizontally based on the axis.
4. Handle duplicate indices carefully during concatenation or joining.
5. Specify keys during concatenation for easier identification of source DataFrames.

Best Practices:

- **Plan Your Strategy:** Choose the appropriate operation based on your data structure and goals.
- **Handle Missing Data:** Use `fillna()` or `dropna()` to manage NaNs introduced during joins or merges.
- **Avoid Redundancy:** Verify column overlaps to prevent duplicate information.
- **Use Descriptive Keys:** When concatenating, use meaningful keys for easier traceability.

- **Test on Subsets:** Perform operations on smaller subsets for validation before applying to the full dataset.

Syntax Table:

SL No	Function/Fe ature	Syntax/Example	Description
1	Merge DataFrames	`pd.merge(df1, df2, on='key')`	Combines DataFrames based on common columns.
2	Join DataFrames	`df1.join(df2, how='left')`	Joins DataFrames on their indices.
3	Concatenate DataFrames	`pd.concat([df1, df2])`	Stacks DataFrames along a specified axis.
4	Concatenate with Keys	`pd.concat([df1, df2], keys=['A', 'B'])`	Adds a hierarchical key to identify sources.
5	Validate Merge	`pd.merge(df1, df2, validate='one_to _one')`	Validates merge expectations.

Syntax Explanation:

1. Merge DataFrames

What is Merging DataFrames?
Combines two DataFrames based on one or more common key columns. This operation is equivalent to SQL joins and supports various join types.
Syntax:
`pd.merge(df1, df2, on='key', how='inner')`

Syntax Explanation:
- **Input DataFrames:** The DataFrames to be merged (df1 and df2).
- **Merge Key:** The column specified in on='key' is used as the basis for merging. If not specified, Pandas attempts to infer common columns.

- **Join Type:** Determines how rows are included:
  - `'inner'`: Includes rows with matching keys in both DataFrames.
  - `'outer'`: Includes all rows, with missing values filled as NaN.
  - `'left'`: Includes all rows from df1 and matching rows from df2.
  - `'right'`: Includes all rows from df2 and matching rows from df1.
- **Suffixes:** Handles overlapping column names by appending specified suffixes (e.g., `'_x'`, `'_y'`).
- Returns a new merged DataFrame with combined columns and rows.

Example:
```
import pandas as pd
# Create DataFrames
data1 = {'ID': [1, 2], 'Name': ['Alice', 'Bob']}
data2 = {'ID': [2, 3], 'Department': ['HR', 'IT']}
df1 = pd.DataFrame(data1)
df2 = pd.DataFrame(data2)
# Merge DataFrames
merged_df = pd.merge(df1, df2, on='ID', how='inner')
print(merged_df)
```

Example Explanation:
- Merges df1 and df2 on the ID column.
- Result: ID Name Department
  0 2 Bob   HR

- This example demonstrates an inner join, retaining rows with matching ID values in both DataFrames.

2. Join DataFrames

What is Joining DataFrames?
Combines two DataFrames on their indices, supporting join operations like left, right, outer, and inner joins.

Syntax:
```
df1.join(df2, how='left')
```

Syntax Explanation:
- **DataFrames:** df1 and df2 are joined based on their indices.
- **Join Types:** Determines how rows are aligned based on index:
    - 'left': Includes all rows from df1.
    - 'right': Includes all rows from df2.
    - 'outer': Includes all rows from both DataFrames, with NaN for missing matches.
    - 'inner': Includes only rows with matching indices.
- **Suffix Handling:** Resolves conflicts by appending specified suffixes to overlapping column names.
- **Alignment:** Index alignment ensures the correct mapping of rows.
- Returns a new joined DataFrame while leaving the originals unchanged.

Example:
```
# Create DataFrames
data1 = {'Name': ['Alice', 'Bob'], 'Age': [25, 30]}
data2 = {'Salary': [50000, 60000]}
df1 = pd.DataFrame(data1, index=['a', 'b'])
df2 = pd.DataFrame(data2, index=['a', 'b'])
# Join DataFrames
joined_df = df1.join(df2)
print(joined_df)
```

Example Explanation:
- Joins df1 and df2 on their indices.
- Result: Name   Age   Salary
    a   Alice   25   50000
    b   Bob   30   60000
- This example demonstrates a default left join, aligning rows based on index.

3. Concatenate DataFrames

What is Concatenating DataFrames?
Stacks DataFrames vertically (default) or horizontally along a specified axis, enabling seamless integration of datasets by rows or columns. This operation is particularly useful for appending new data, consolidating datasets, or aligning complementary attributes for analysis.

Syntax:
```
pd.concat([df1, df2], axis=0)
```

Syntax Explanation:
- **Input:** A list of DataFrames [df1, df2] to concatenate. These can have matching or differing column structures.
- **Axis:**
  - axis=0: Stacks rows vertically.
  - axis=1: Combines columns horizontally.
- **Index Handling:**
  - ignore_index=True: Resets the index in the resulting DataFrame.
  - keys: Creates a hierarchical index to identify data sources.
- **Preservation:** Maintains original DataFrames unless explicitly modified.

Example:
```
# Create DataFrames
data1 = {'Name': ['Alice'], 'Age': [25]}
data2 = {'Name': ['Bob'], 'Age': [30]}
df1 = pd.DataFrame(data1)
df2 = pd.DataFrame(data2)
# Concatenate DataFrames
concat_df = pd.concat([df1, df2], ignore_index=True)
print(concat_df)
```

Example Explanation:
- Concatenates df1 and df2 vertically.
- Result: Name   Age
  ```
  0   Alice    25
  1     Bob    30
  ```
- Simplifies combining data with identical structures.

4. Concatenate with Keys

What is Concatenating with Keys?
Adds hierarchical keys to identify source DataFrames in the concatenated result, providing a clear structure for tracing the origin of data entries. This feature is particularly beneficial when combining multiple datasets for analysis, as it simplifies data source tracking and enhances organizational clarity.

Syntax:
```
pd.concat([df1, df2], keys=['A', 'B'])
```

Syntax Explanation:
- **Input:** A list of DataFrames [df1, df2] to concatenate.
- **Keys:** Assigns labels to the source DataFrames, creating a hierarchical index.
- **Axis:** Defaults to axis=0 for vertical stacking.
- **Hierarchical Indexing:** Facilitates better tracking of data origins in the combined result.

Example:
```
# Concatenate with keys
concat_df = pd.concat([df1, df2], keys=['Group1',
'Group2'])
print(concat_df)
```

Example Explanation:
- Result: Name   Age
  ```
  Group1 0   Alice    25
  Group2 0     Bob    30
  ```

- Hierarchical keys clarify data provenance.

5. Validate Merge

What is Validating a Merge?
Ensures the merging operation adheres to expected relationships, such as one-to-one or one-to-many mappings.
Syntax:
```
pd.merge(df1, df2, on='key', validate='one_to_one')
```

Syntax Explanation:
- **Validation Types:**
    - `'one_to_one'`: Ensures no duplicate keys in either DataFrame.
    - `'one_to_many'`: Allows duplicates in the right DataFrame.
    - `'many_to_one'`: Allows duplicates in the left DataFrame.
- **Error Handling:** Raises an error if the specified relationship is violated.
- Enhances reliability in merging operations.

Example:
```
# Merge with validation
validated_df = pd.merge(df1, df2, on='ID',
validate='one_to_one')
print(validated_df)
```

Example Explanation:
- Ensures a one-to-one relationship between df1 and df2.

Real-Life Project:

Project Name: Employee Database Consolidation
Project Goal:
Combine employee information from different departments into a single comprehensive database.

Code for This Project:

```python
import pandas as pd
# Create department DataFrames
data_hr = {'ID': [1, 2], 'Name': ['Alice', 'Bob'],
'Department': ['HR', 'HR']}
data_it = {'ID': [3, 4], 'Name': ['Charlie', 'David'],
'Department': ['IT', 'IT']}
hr_df = pd.DataFrame(data_hr)
it_df = pd.DataFrame(data_it)


# Concatenate DataFrames
all_employees = pd.concat([hr_df, it_df], keys=['HR',
'IT'])
print("Consolidated Employee Database:\n",
all_employees)
```

Expanded Features:
- Combines multiple datasets with hierarchical keys.
- Tracks data origins clearly.

Expected Output:

```
      ID     Name Department
HR 0   1    Alice        HR
HR 1   2      Bob        HR
IT 0   3  Charlie        IT
IT 1   4    David        IT
```

Chapter-17 Reshaping and Pivoting DataFrames in Pandas

Reshaping and pivoting are essential operations in data analysis, allowing you to transform data into the desired structure for analysis or visualization. Pandas provides a range of tools to reshape and reorganize data efficiently, including pivoting, stacking, unstacking, and melting. This chapter explores these methods in depth, with examples and practical applications.

Key Characteristics of Reshaping and Pivoting:

- **Flexibility:** Supports transforming data between wide and long formats.
- **Integration:** Works seamlessly with other Pandas operations like grouping and aggregation.
- **Ease of Use:** Intuitive syntax for complex reshaping tasks.
- **Efficiency:** Optimized for large datasets, ensuring quick transformations.

Basic Rules for Reshaping and Pivoting:

1. Use pivot for reshaping data based on unique index/column combinations.
2. Use melt to convert wide-format data into long-format data.
3. Handle missing values when reshaping with fillna() or by defining default values.
4. Ensure the index/column structure is appropriate for the desired transformation.
5. Combine reshaping with grouping or aggregation for advanced data manipulation.

Best Practices:

- **Plan the Final Structure:** Decide the desired data format before applying transformations.
- **Handle Duplicates:** Ensure no duplicate index/column combinations exist for operations like pivot.
- **Use Clear Naming:** Rename columns and indices after reshaping for clarity.
- **Leverage Visualization:** Reshaped data often provides better

insights when visualized.

- **Combine Operations:** Integrate reshaping with filtering, grouping, or sorting for comprehensive data preparation.

Syntax Table:

SL No	Function/ Feature	Syntax/Example	Description
1	Pivot Table	`df.pivot(index, columns, values)`	Reshapes data into a pivot table.
2	Melt	`df.melt(id_vars, value_vars)`	Converts wide-format data into long format.
3	Stack	`df.stack()`	Stacks columns into a multi-level index.
4	Unstack	`df.unstack(level)`	Unstacks rows into columns.
5	Transpose	`df.T`	Transposes rows and columns.

Syntax Explanation:

1. Pivot Table

What is Pivot Table?

A pivot table reshapes data by aggregating values based on specified rows and columns. It's ideal for summarizing and analyzing datasets.

Syntax:

`df.pivot(index='row', columns='column', values='value')`

Syntax Explanation:

- index: Specifies the rows in the pivot table.
- columns: Specifies the columns in the pivot table.
- values: Defines the data values to aggregate.
- The method requires unique combinations of index and columns. Duplicate values raise an error.
- Returns a reshaped DataFrame with rows and columns arranged based on the specified arguments.

`Example:`

```python
import pandas as pd
# Create a DataFrame
data = {
    'City': ['NY', 'LA', 'NY'],
    'Product': ['A', 'A', 'B'],
    'Sales': [100, 200, 150]
}
df = pd.DataFrame(data)
pivot_table = df.pivot(index='City', columns='Product',
values='Sales')
print(pivot_table)
```

Example Explanation:

- Groups sales data by city and product.
- Result: Product   A   B
  City
  LA   200.0 NaN
  NY   100.0 150.0
- This structure simplifies comparisons across cities and products.

2. Melt

What is Melt?

Melt transforms wide-format data into long-format data, making it easier to analyze or visualize.

Syntax:

```python
df.melt(id_vars=['id'], value_vars=['col1', 'col2'])
```

Syntax Explanation:

- id_vars: Specifies columns to keep as identifiers.
- value_vars: Defines columns to unpivot into rows.
- The resulting DataFrame has columns for id_vars, variable names, and values.
- This method is particularly useful for preparing data for plotting or statistical analysis.

Example:

```python
# Melt a DataFrame
```

```
data = {
    'City': ['NY', 'LA'],
    'A_Sales': [100, 200],
    'B_Sales': [150, 250]
}
df = pd.DataFrame(data)
melted = df.melt(id_vars='City', value_vars=['A_Sales',
'B_Sales'], var_name='Product', value_name='Sales')
print(melted)
```

Example Explanation:

- Transforms columns A_Sales and B_Sales into rows.
- Result: City Product Sales
    0 NY A_Sales 100
    1 LA A_Sales 200
    2 NY B_Sales 150
    3 LA B_Sales 250

- This structure facilitates analysis or visualization.

3. Stack

What is Stack?
Stack transforms columns into rows, creating a multi-level index for better organization.
Syntax:
```
df.stack(level=-1)
```

Syntax Explanation:
- level: Specifies the level to stack. Default is -1 (innermost level).
- The method reshapes columns into rows, adding a new level to the DataFrame index.
- Useful for compacting wide tables into hierarchical row formats.

Example:

```
# Stack a DataFrame
data = {
    'A': [1, 2],
    'B': [3, 4]
}
df = pd.DataFrame(data, index=['row1', 'row2'])
stacked = df.stack()
print(stacked)
```

Example Explanation:

- Stacks columns A and B into rows.
- Result: row1 A   1
     B   3
  row2 A   2
     B   4
  dtype: int64
- Enhances data organization for hierarchical analysis.

4. Unstack

What is Unstack?

Unstack performs the reverse operation of stack, converting rows into columns.

Syntax:

```
df.unstack(level=-1)
```

Syntax Explanation:
- level: Specifies the index level to unstack. Default is -1 (innermost level).
- Converts part of the row index into column labels.
- Useful for expanding hierarchical row data into columns.

Example:
```
# Unstack a DataFrame
```

```
stacked = df.stack()
unstacked = stacked.unstack()
print(unstacked)
```

Example Explanation:
- Reverses the stacking operation.
- Restores the original wide format of the DataFrame.

5. Transpose

What is Transpose?
Transpose switches rows and columns, providing a quick way to reorganize data.

Syntax:
```
df.T
```

Syntax Explanation:
- The T attribute flips rows and columns.
- Useful for swapping dimensions to view data differently.
- Works efficiently on DataFrames of any size.

Example:
```
# Transpose a DataFrame
data = {
    'Name': ['Alice', 'Bob'],
    'Age': [25, 30]
}
df = pd.DataFrame(data)
transposed = df.T
print(transposed)
```

Example Explanation:
- Switches rows and columns.
- Result: 0   1
  Name Alice   Bob
  Age   25   30
- Useful for quickly flipping data orientations.

Real-Life Project:

Project Name: Sales Data Transformation
Project Goal:
Prepare a sales dataset by reshaping and pivoting it for analysis and visualization.
Code for This Project:

```python
import pandas as pd
# Create sales data
data = {
    'Region': ['North', 'South', 'North', 'South'],
    'Product': ['A', 'A', 'B', 'B'],
    'Sales': [100, 200, 150, 250]
}
df = pd.DataFrame(data)

# Pivot the data
pivot_df = df.pivot(index='Region', columns='Product',
values='Sales')

# Melt the data
melted_df =
pivot_df.reset_index().melt(id_vars='Region',
var_name='Product', value_name='Sales')

print("Pivoted Data:\n", pivot_df)
print("Melted Data:\n", melted_df)
```

Expected Output:
```
Pivoted Data:
Product      A      B
Region
North      100    150
South      200    250
```

Part 4: Data Analysis with Pandas

Chapter-18 Exploratory Data Analysis (EDA) with Pandas

Exploratory Data Analysis (EDA) is a crucial step in understanding your dataset, identifying patterns, detecting anomalies, and forming hypotheses. Pandas provides a comprehensive suite of tools for conducting EDA efficiently. This chapter delves into essential techniques for summarizing, visualizing, and analyzing data using Pandas.

Key Characteristics of EDA with Pandas:

- **Versatility:** Supports diverse operations like summarization, filtering, and aggregation.
- **Integration:** Works seamlessly with libraries like Matplotlib and Seaborn for enhanced visualizations.
- **Efficiency:** Handles large datasets effectively with optimized operations.
- **Flexibility:** Provides tools for both numerical and categorical data analysis.

Basic Rules for EDA:

1. Start by understanding the data structure with methods like `info()` and `head()`.
2. Handle missing values early using `fillna()` or `dropna()`.
3. Summarize numerical data using descriptive statistics.
4. Visualize data distributions and relationships to identify patterns.
5. Iterate on insights by combining filtering, grouping, and aggregation.

Best Practices:

- **Know Your Data:** Familiarize yourself with the dataset's columns, types, and values.
- **Clean as You Explore:** Address missing values, duplicates, and outliers.
- **Leverage Visualizations:** Combine numerical summaries with plots for better insights.
- **Document Findings:** Record observations for better decision-

making.

- **Test Assumptions:** Use visual and numerical methods to validate hypotheses.

Syntax Table:

SL No	Function/Feature	Syntax/Example	Description
1	Data Overview	`df.info()`	Provides a summary of the dataset.
2	Summary Statistics	`df.describe()`	Generates descriptive statistics.
3	Value Counts	`df['column'].value_counts()`	Counts unique values in a column.
4	Correlation Matrix	`df.corr()`	Computes pairwise correlation coefficients.
5	Grouping and Aggregation	`df.groupby('column').agg(func)`	Summarizes data by groups.

Syntax Explanation:

1. Data Overview

What is Data Overview?

Provides a high-level summary of the dataset, including column names, non-null counts, and data types.

Syntax:

```
df.info()
```

Syntax Explanation:

- df: The target DataFrame.
- Returns column names, data types, and memory usage.
- Helps identify missing values and understand dataset dimensions.

Example:

```
import pandas as pd
# Create a DataFrame
data = {'Name': ['Alice', 'Bob', 'Charlie'], 'Age':
[25, 30, None]}
df = pd.DataFrame(data)
df.info()
```

Example Explanation:
- Outputs: `<class 'pandas.core.frame.DataFrame'>`

  ```
  RangeIndex: 3 entries, 0 to 2
  Data columns (total 2 columns):
   #   Column  Non-Null Count  Dtype
  ---  ------  --------------  -----
   0   Name    3 non-null      object
   1   Age     2 non-null      float64
  dtypes: float64(1), object(1)
  memory usage: 176.0+ bytes
  ```

- Highlights missing values in the Age column.

2. Summary Statistics

What is Summary Statistics?

Provides a summary of numerical columns, including mean, median, and standard deviation.

Syntax:
```
df.describe()
```

Syntax Explanation:
- df: The target DataFrame.
- Includes summary metrics such as count, mean, min, max, and quartiles.
- Excludes non-numerical columns by default unless specified with `include='all'`.
- Useful for understanding data distributions.

Example:
```
# Generate descriptive statistics
data = {'Age': [25, 30, 35, 40], 'Salary': [50000,
60000, 55000, 70000]}
df = pd.DataFrame(data)
print(df.describe())
```

Example Explanation:

- Outputs:

```
              Age           Salary
count     4.000000        4.000000
mean     32.500000    58750.000000
std       6.454972     8539.125638
min      25.000000    50000.000000
25%      28.750000    53750.000000
50%      32.500000    57500.000000
75%      36.250000    62500.000000
max      40.000000    70000.000000
```

- Summarizes numerical columns for quick insights.

3. Value Counts

What is Value Counts?

Counts the occurrences of unique values in a column.

Syntax:

```
df['column'].value_counts(normalize=False)
```

Syntax Explanation:

- `df['column']`: Specifies the target column.
- `normalize=False`: Returns absolute counts by default. Set to True for proportions.
- Sorted in descending order by count.
- Useful for analyzing categorical variables.

Example:

```
# Count unique values
data = {'City': ['NY', 'LA', 'NY', 'SF']}
df = pd.DataFrame(data)
print(df['City'].value_counts())
```

Example Explanation:

- Outputs:

```
NY    2
LA    1
SF    1
Name: City, dtype: int64
```

- Highlights the frequency of each city.

4. Correlation Matrix

What is Correlation Matrix?
Calculates the pairwise correlation coefficients between numerical columns.

Syntax:
```
df.corr(method='pearson')
```

Syntax Explanation:
- `df`: The target DataFrame.
- `method`: Specifies the correlation method (`'pearson'`, `'kendall'`, or `'spearman'`).
- Returns a DataFrame with correlation coefficients ranging from -1 to 1.
- Useful for understanding relationships between variables.

Example:
```
# Compute correlation matrix
data = {'Age': [25, 30, 35], 'Salary': [50000, 60000, 55000]}
df = pd.DataFrame(data)
print(df.corr())
```

Example Explanation:
- Outputs:
  ```
              Age       Salary
  Age     1.000000    0.500000
  Salary  0.500000    1.000000
  ```

- Reveals a moderate positive correlation between Age and Salary.

5. Grouping and Aggregation

What is Grouping and Aggregation?

Groups data based on a column and applies aggregate functions to summarize values.

.

Syntax:

```
df.groupby('column').agg({'col1': 'mean', 'col2':
'sum'})
```

Syntax Explanation:
- df.groupby('column'): Groups rows by unique values in the specified column.
- agg: Applies specified aggregation functions to target columns.
- Returns a summarized DataFrame with grouped rows and aggregated values.

Example:
```
# Group and aggregate
data = {'City': ['NY', 'LA', 'NY'], 'Sales': [100, 200,
150]}
df = pd.DataFrame(data)
result = df.groupby('City').sum()
print(result)
```

Example Explanation:
- Outputs: Sales
  City
  LA   200
  NY   250

- Summarizes total sales by city.

Real-Life Project:

Project Name: Customer Purchase Analysis
Project Goal:
Perform EDA to uncover insights into customer purchasing behavior.

Code for This Project:
```
import pandas as pd
# Create purchase data
data = {
    'CustomerID': [1, 2, 3, 4],
    'Product': ['A', 'B', 'A', 'C'],
    'Amount': [50, 100, 75, 200]
}
df = pd.DataFrame(data)

# Data Overview
df.info()

# Summary Statistics
print(df.describe())

# Value Counts
print(df['Product'].value_counts())

# Grouping and Aggregation
summary = df.groupby('Product').agg({'Amount': 'sum'})
print("Sales by Product:\n", summary)
```

Expanded Features:
- Combines multiple EDA techniques for a comprehensive analysis.
- Highlights key metrics and trends in purchasing behavior.

Expected Output:

```
<class 'pandas.core.frame.DataFrame'>
RangeIndex: 4 entries, 0 to 3
Data columns (total 3 columns):
 #   Column      Non-Null Count  Dtype
---  ------      --------------  -----
 0   CustomerID  4 non-null      int64
 1   Product     4 non-null      object
 2   Amount      4 non-null      int64
dtypes: int64(2), object(1)
```

```
memory usage: 224.0 bytes

        Amount
count     4.00
mean    106.25
std      68.45
min      50.00
25%      68.
```

Chapter-18 Descriptive Statistics in Pandas

Descriptive statistics are essential for summarizing and understanding the main characteristics of a dataset. Pandas provides a wide range of tools to compute these statistics efficiently. This chapter explores various methods to measure central tendency, dispersion, and distribution properties, enabling data scientists to gain valuable insights from data.

Key Characteristics of Descriptive Statistics in Pandas:

- **Comprehensive Methods:** Supports a variety of statistical measures including mean, median, mode, variance, and standard deviation.
- **Ease of Use:** Offers simple, chainable methods for quick computation.
- **Flexibility:** Handles both numerical and categorical data.
- **Performance:** Optimized for efficient computations on large datasets.
- **Integration:** Works seamlessly with data preprocessing workflows.

Basic Rules for Descriptive Statistics:

1. Statistics can be computed for entire DataFrames, specific columns, or grouped subsets.
2. Missing values are excluded by default unless explicitly handled.
3. Results can often be returned as scalar values or DataFrames, depending on the input.
4. Operations are vectorized, ensuring efficient computation.

Best Practices:

- **Inspect Data First:** Use methods like df.info() and df.describe() to get an overview of the dataset.

- **Handle Missing Values:** Address missing data with fillna() or dropna() before computing statistics.
- **Use Grouping:** Combine with groupby() for category-wise statistics.
- **Select Relevant Columns:** Filter columns for focused analysis.
- **Visualize Results:** Complement descriptive statistics with data visualization for deeper insights.

Syntax Table:

SL No	Function/Feature	Syntax/Example	Description
1	Summary Statistics	`df.describe()`	Computes summary statistics for numeric columns.
2	Mean	`df['column'].mean()`	Computes the mean of a column.
3	Median	`df['column'].median()`	Computes the median of a column.
4	Variance	`df['column'].var()`	Computes the variance of a column.
5	Standard Deviation	`df['column'].std()`	Computes the standard deviation of a column.

Syntax Explanation:

1. Summary Statistics

What is Summary Statistics?

Computes descriptive statistics for all numeric columns, providing a quick overview of key metrics like count, mean, min, max, and quartiles.

Syntax:

`df.describe()`

Syntax Explanation:

- df: The input DataFrame.
- Includes numeric columns by default. Set include='all' to include all columns, including categorical data.
- Returns a DataFrame with aggregated metrics for each column.
- Excludes missing values by default.

Example:
```
import pandas as pd
# Create a DataFrame
data = {'Name': ['Alice', 'Bob', 'Charlie'], 'Age':
[25, 30, 35], 'Salary': [50000, 60000, 70000]}
df = pd.DataFrame(data)
summary = df.describe()
print("Summary Statistics:\n", summary)
```

Example Explanation:

- Outputs summary statistics for Age and Salary

```
columns:           Age         Salary
count    3.000      3.000000
mean    30.000  60000.000000
std      5.000  10000.000000
min     25.000  50000.000000
25%     27.500  55000.000000
50%     30.000  60000.000000
75%     32.500  65000.000000
max     35.000  70000.000000
```

2. Mean
What is Mean?
Calculates the average value of a numeric column.
Syntax:
```
df['column'].mean()
```

Syntax Explanation:
- df['column']: Specifies the column to compute the mean.
- Returns a scalar value representing the arithmetic mean.
- Excludes NaN values by default.

Example:
```
mean_age = df['Age'].mean()
print("Mean Age:", mean_age)
```

Example Explanation:
- Computes the average of the Age column.
- Outputs: 30.0.

3. Median
What is Median?

Finds the middle value of a numeric column when sorted in ascending order.

Syntax:
```
df['column'].median()
```

Syntax Explanation:
- df['column']: Specifies the column to compute the median.
- Returns a scalar value representing the median.
- Automatically handles odd and even numbers of elements by computing the middle or average of the two middle values.

Example:
```
median_salary = df['Salary'].median()
print("Median Salary:", median_salary)
```

Example Explanation:
- Computes the median of the Salary column.
- Outputs: 60000.0.

4. Variance
What is Variance?

Measures the spread of data in a column by calculating the average squared deviation from the mean.

Syntax:
```
df['column'].var()
```

Syntax Explanation:

- df['column']: Specifies the column to compute the variance.
- Returns a scalar value representing the variance.
- Excludes missing values by default.
- Useful for assessing data dispersion.

Example:
```
variance_salary = df['Salary'].var()
print("Variance of Salary:", variance_salary)
```

Example Explanation:

- Computes the variance of the Salary column.
- Outputs: 100000000.0.

5. Standard Deviation

What is Standard Deviation?

Quantifies the amount of variation in a dataset by computing the square root of the variance.

Syntax:
```
df['column'].std()
```

Syntax Explanation:

- df['column']: Specifies the column to compute the standard deviation.
- Returns a scalar value representing the standard deviation.
- Indicates how much individual data points deviate from the mean.

Example:
```
std_salary = df['Salary'].std()
print("Standard Deviation of Salary:", std_salary)
```

Example Explanation:

- Computes the standard deviation of the Salary column.
- Outputs: 10000.0.

Real-Life Project:

Project Name: Employee Performance Analysis

Project Goal:

Use descriptive statistics to analyze employee performance metrics such as age, salary, and productivity scores.

Code for This Project:

```python
import pandas as pd
# Create a DataFrame with employee data
employee_data = {
    'EmployeeID': [1, 2, 3, 4],
    'Name': ['Alice', 'Bob', 'Charlie', 'David'],
    'Age': [25, 30, 35, 40],
    'Salary': [50000, 60000, 70000, 80000],
    'ProductivityScore': [80, 85, 90, 95]
}
df = pd.DataFrame(employee_data)

# Compute key statistics
mean_salary = df['Salary'].mean()
median_age = df['Age'].median()
std_productivity = df['ProductivityScore'].std()

print("Mean Salary:", mean_salary)
print("Median Age:", median_age)
print("Standard Deviation of Productivity Score:",
std_productivity)
```

Expanded Features:
- Demonstrates multiple descriptive statistics methods.
- Highlights practical applications in real-world analysis.
- Provides insights for HR decisions and policy-making.

Expected Output:

Mean Salary: 65000.0

Median Age: 32.5

Standard Deviation of Productivity Score: 7.5

Chapter-19 Correlation and Covariance in Pandas

Correlation and covariance are fundamental statistical measures used to understand relationships between variables in a dataset. Pandas provides simple and efficient methods to calculate these metrics, helping data analysts and scientists uncover insights into how variables interact with one another.

Key Characteristics of Correlation and Covariance in Pandas:

- **Comprehensive Methods:** Supports pairwise and matrix-level computations for both correlation and covariance.
- **Ease of Use:** Provides intuitive methods for quick calculations.
- **Flexible Input:** Handles DataFrames and Series seamlessly.
- **Performance:** Optimized for efficient computations on large datasets.
- **Integration:** Works well with other Pandas functions for advanced analysis.

Basic Rules for Correlation and Covariance:

1. Correlation measures the strength and direction of a linear relationship between variables (range: -1 to 1).
2. Covariance measures the degree to which two variables change together.
3. Both methods exclude missing values by default.
4. Pairwise correlation and covariance matrices are computed for numeric columns only.

Best Practices:

- **Understand the Context:** Use correlation for linear relationships and covariance for general co-variability.
- **Handle Missing Data:** Ensure missing values are handled appropriately using methods like fillna() or dropna().
- **Visualize Relationships:** Pair calculations with scatter plots or heatmaps for better interpretation.
- **Focus on Numeric Data:** Filter non-numeric columns for accurate results.
- **Combine with Grouping:** Use groupby() for category-specific analysis of correlations and covariances.

Syntax Table:

SL No	Function/Feature	Syntax/Example	Description
1	Pairwise Correlation	`df.corr()`	Computes correlation matrix for all numeric columns.
2	Pairwise Covariance	`df.cov()`	Computes covariance matrix for all numeric columns.
3	Series Correlation	`series1.corr(series2)`	Computes correlation between two Series.
4	Series Covariance	`series1.cov(series2)`	Computes covariance between two Series.
5	Correlation with Method	`df.corr(method='spearman')`	Computes correlation using a specific method.

Syntax Explanation:

1. Pairwise Correlation

What is Pairwise Correlation?

Computes the correlation matrix for all numeric columns in a DataFrame.

Syntax:

`df.corr()`

Syntax Explanation:

- df: The input DataFrame.
- Calculates Pearson correlation coefficients by default.
- Returns a DataFrame with pairwise correlation coefficients for all numeric columns.
- Excludes non-numeric columns and missing values automatically.
- Supports specifying alternative correlation methods like Spearman or Kendall using the method parameter.

Example:

```
import pandas as pd
# Create a DataFrame
data = {'A': [1, 2, 3], 'B': [4, 5, 6], 'C': [7, 8,
10]}
df = pd.DataFrame(data)
correlation_matrix = df.corr()
```

```
print("Correlation Matrix:\n", correlation_matrix)
```

Example Explanation:

- Computes correlations between columns A, B, and C.
- Outputs:

```
         A      B     C
A  1.000   1.0   0.98
B  1.000   1.0   0.98
C  0.980  0.98   1.00
```

- Indicates strong positive correlations between all columns.

2. Pairwise Covariance

What is Pairwise Covariance?

Computes the covariance matrix for all numeric columns in a DataFrame.

Syntax:

```
df.cov()
```

Syntax Explanation:

- df: The input DataFrame.
- Measures the degree to which numeric columns vary together.
- Returns a DataFrame with pairwise covariance values.
- Automatically excludes non-numeric columns and missing values.

Example:

```
covariance_matrix = df.cov()
print("Covariance Matrix:\n", covariance_matrix)
```

Example Explanation:

- Computes covariances between columns A, B, and C.
- Outputs:

```
         A       B      C
A  1.000   1.000   0.950
B  1.000   1.000   0.950
C  0.950   0.950   1.025
```

- Shows how columns co-vary in their values.

3. Series Correlation

What is Series Correlation?

Computes the correlation between two Series.

Syntax:
```
series1.corr(series2)
```

Syntax Explanation:
- series1 and series2: The two Series objects to compare.
- Calculates Pearson correlation coefficient by default.
- Returns a scalar value representing the correlation.

Example:
```
series1 = pd.Series([1, 2, 3])
series2 = pd.Series([4, 5, 6])
correlation = series1.corr(series2)
print("Correlation:", correlation)
```

Example Explanation:
- Computes the correlation between series1 and series2.
- Outputs: 1.0, indicating a perfect positive linear relationship.

4. Series Covariance

What is Series Covariance?
Computes the covariance between two Series.

Syntax:
```
series1.cov(series2)
```

Syntax Explanation:

- series1 and series2: The two Series objects to compare.
- Returns a scalar value representing the covariance.
- Excludes missing values by default.

Example:

```
covariance = series1.cov(series2)
print("Covariance:", covariance)
```

Example Explanation:

- Computes the covariance between series1 and series2.
- Outputs: 1.0, showing how the two Series vary together.

5. Correlation with Method

What is Correlation with Method?

Calculates correlation using a specified method (Pearson, Spearman, or Kendall).

Syntax:

```
df.corr(method='spearman')
```

Syntax Explanation:

- method: Specifies the correlation method ('pearson' for linear, 'spearman' for rank-based, 'kendall' for ordinal relationships).
- Returns a DataFrame with correlation coefficients based on the selected method.
- Useful for non-linear or ranked relationships.

Example:

```
spearman_corr = df.corr(method='spearman')
print("Spearman Correlation:\n", spearman_corr)
```

Example Explanation:

- Computes Spearman rank correlation.
- Outputs a correlation matrix, useful for ranked or monotonic relationships.

Real-Life Project:

Project Name: Stock Price Analysis
Project Goal:
Analyze the correlation and covariance between the prices of different stocks to understand market trends and relationships.

Code for This Project:

```python
import pandas as pd
# Create a DataFrame with stock prices
data = {
    'Stock_A': [100, 102, 104, 108],
    'Stock_B': [200, 202, 206, 210],
    'Stock_C': [300, 305, 310, 315]
}
df = pd.DataFrame(data)

# Compute correlation and covariance
correlation_matrix = df.corr()
covariance_matrix = df.cov()

print("Correlation Matrix:\n", correlation_matrix)
print("Covariance Matrix:\n", covariance_matrix)
```

Expanded Features:

- Demonstrates correlation and covariance analysis for financial data.
- Highlights pairwise relationships among multiple variables.
- Provides insights into stock price trends and co-movement.

Expected Output:

```
Correlation Matrix:
          Stock_A   Stock_B   Stock_C
Stock_A     1.0       1.0       1.0
Stock_B     1.0       1.0       1.0
Stock_C     1.0       1.0       1.0
Covariance Matrix:
          Stock_A   Stock_B   Stock_C
Stock_A    16.0      16.0      16.0
Stock_B    16.0      16.0      16.0
Stock_C    16.0      16.0      16.0
```

This project demonstrates how to compute and interpret correlation and covariance in financial datasets for better decision-making and trend analysis.

Chapter-20 Handling Time Series Data in Pandas

Time series data is a sequence of data points indexed in time order. Pandas provides robust tools to manipulate, analyze, and visualize time series data efficiently. This chapter explores essential techniques for handling datetime indices, resampling, shifting, and performing rolling calculations, enabling users to extract meaningful insights from temporal datasets.

Key Characteristics of Time Series in Pandas:

- **Datetime Indexing:** Efficient handling of datetime objects as indices.
- **Resampling and Frequency Conversion:** Flexible tools for upsampling and downsampling data.
- **Shifting and Lagging:** Enables time-based data alignment for comparison.
- **Rolling and Expanding Calculations:** Supports moving averages and other statistical operations.
- **Integration:** Seamlessly integrates with other Pandas operations and libraries like Matplotlib.

Basic Rules for Handling Time Series Data:

1. Time series data requires a datetime-like index for efficient manipulation.
2. Use pd.to_datetime() to convert strings to datetime objects.
3. Resampling, shifting, and rolling operations require specifying time-based frequencies.
4. Time zones can be managed with methods like tz_localize() and tz_convert().

Best Practices:

- **Ensure Proper Indexing:** Always set a datetime-like index for time series data.
- **Leverage Resampling:** Aggregate data to meaningful time intervals for analysis.
- **Handle Missing Data:** Use interpolation or fill methods for gaps in time series.

- **Visualize Patterns:** Use line plots or seasonal decomposition to identify trends.
- **Combine with Aggregations:** Use rolling or expanding methods for deeper insights.

Syntax Table:

SL No	Function/Feature	Syntax/Example	Description
1	Convert to Datetime	`pd.to_datetime(df['column'])`	Converts strings to datetime objects.
2	Set Datetime Index	`df.set_index('datetime_column')`	Sets a column as the datetime index.
3	Resampling	`df.resample('M').mean()`	Aggregates data to specified frequency.
4	Shifting Data	`df.shift(1)`	Shifts data by a specified number of periods.
5	Rolling Calculations	`df.rolling(window=3).mean()`	Computes rolling statistics.

Syntax Explanation:

1. Convert to Datetime

What is Convert to Datetime?
Converts strings or other objects into datetime objects for time series analysis.

Syntax:
`pd.to_datetime(df['column'])`

Syntax Explanation:

- df['column']: Specifies the column containing datetime-like values.
- Automatically infers datetime format or allows specifying it with the format parameter.
- Handles invalid parsing with the errors parameter ('coerce', 'raise', 'ignore').
- Returns a Series of datetime objects compatible with time-based

operations.

Example:

```
import pandas as pd
data = {'date': ['2023-01-01', '2023-01-02', '2023-01-
03']}
df = pd.DataFrame(data)
df['date'] = pd.to_datetime(df['date'])
print(df)
```

Example Explanation:

- Converts the date column to datetime objects.
- Outputs: date
  0 2023-01-01
  1 2023-01-02
  2 2023-01-03

2. Set Datetime Index

What is Set Datetime Index?
Sets a datetime column as the index of a DataFrame to enable time-based operations.
Syntax:
```
df.set_index('datetime_column')
```

Syntax Explanation:

- datetime_column: Specifies the column to set as the index.
- Allows efficient slicing, filtering, and resampling by datetime values.
- Can be chained with pd.to_datetime() for direct conversion and indexing.
- Returns a new DataFrame with the datetime index unless inplace=True is specified.

Example:

```
df.set_index('date', inplace=True)
print(df)
```

Example Explanation:
- Sets the date column as the index.
- Outputs:

  2023-01-01
  2023-01-02
  2023-01-03

3. Resampling

What is Resampling?
Aggregates data to a specified frequency, such as daily, monthly, or yearly intervals.

Syntax:

```
df.resample('M').mean()
```

Syntax Explanation:
- 'M': Specifies the resampling frequency (e.g., 'D' for daily, 'H' for hourly).
- mean(): The aggregation function applied to resampled data (e.g., sum(), count(), etc.).
- Returns a resampled DataFrame or Series with the specified frequency.
- Handles gaps in data by inserting NaN values for missing periods.

Example:

```
resampled = df.resample('M').mean()
print(resampled)
```

Example Explanation:
- Aggregates data to monthly intervals, computing the mean for each interval.
- Outputs a resampled DataFrame with monthly averages.

4. Shifting Data

What is Shifting Data?
Moves data forward or backward by a specified number of periods.
Syntax:
```
df.shift(periods=1)
```

Syntax Explanation:
- periods: Specifies the number of periods to shift (positive for forward, negative for backward).
- Shifts both index and data values, introducing NaNs for out-of-bound entries.
- Useful for creating lagged or lead features in time series analysis.

Example:
```
shifted = df.shift(1)
print(shifted)
```

Example Explanation:
- Shifts data forward by one period.
- Outputs a DataFrame with NaN in the first row and all other rows shifted down.

5. Rolling Calculations

What is Rolling Calculations?
Applies a statistical function over a moving window of specified size.
Syntax:
```
df.rolling(window=3).mean()
```

Syntax Explanation:

- window: The size of the moving window (e.g., 3 for a 3-period rolling calculation).
- mean(): The function applied to the rolling window (e.g., sum(), std(), etc.).
- Returns a DataFrame or Series with rolling statistics.
- Introduces NaN values for periods where the full window size is not available.

Example:

```
rolling_avg = df['column'].rolling(window=3).mean()
print(rolling_avg)
```

Example Explanation:

- Computes the rolling average over a 3-period window.
- Outputs a Series with NaN for the first two rows and rolling averages thereafter.

Real-Life Project:

Project Name: Sales Trend Analysis
Project Goal:
Analyze daily sales data to identify trends, seasonality, and anomalies.
Code for This Project:

```
import pandas as pd
# Create a sales DataFrame
data = {
    'date': ['2023-01-01', '2023-01-02', '2023-01-03',
'2023-01-04'],
    'sales': [200, 220, 210, 230]
}
df = pd.DataFrame(data)
df['date'] = pd.to_datetime(df['date'])
df.set_index('date', inplace=True)
```

```python
# Resample to weekly sales
weekly_sales = df.resample('W').sum()

# Compute rolling average
rolling_avg = df['sales'].rolling(window=2).mean()

print("Weekly Sales:\n", weekly_sales)
print("Rolling Average:\n", rolling_avg)
```

Expanded Features:
- Demonstrates conversion, indexing, resampling, and rolling calculations.
- Highlights methods to extract trends and smooth out fluctuations.
- Useful for business reporting and decision-making.

Expected Output:
```
Weekly Sales:
            sales
2023-01-08   860

Rolling Average:
2023-01-01    NaN
2023-01-02    210.0
2023-01-03    215.0
2023-01-04    220.0
```

This project showcases practical techniques for handling and analyzing time series data in Pandas.

Chapter-21 Working with Categorical Data in Pandas

Categorical data represents variables with a fixed number of categories or groups, such as gender, color, or product types. Pandas provides robust tools to handle categorical data efficiently, offering memory optimization and enhanced performance for common operations like sorting, filtering, and aggregations. This chapter explores how to define, manipulate, and analyze categorical data in Pandas.

Key Characteristics of Categorical Data in Pandas:

- **Memory Efficiency:** Stores data as integer codes instead of strings.
- **Performance Boost:** Accelerates operations like comparisons and sorting.
- **Categorical Methods:** Offers specific methods for working with categories.
- **Custom Categories:** Allows defining ordered and unordered categories.
- **Integration:** Works seamlessly with other Pandas functionality.

Basic Rules for Categorical Data:

1. Use pd.Categorical or astype('category') to define categorical data.
2. Categories can be unordered (default) or ordered for ranked data.
3. Missing categories can be added using the categories parameter.
4. Categorical data improves performance for repetitive string comparisons.
5. Aggregation and grouping are more efficient with categorical variables.

Best Practices:

- **Define Categories Early:** Convert columns to categorical type during data loading or preprocessing.
- **Optimize Memory:** Use categorical data for columns with a limited number of unique values.
- **Leverage Ordered Categories:** Use ordered categories for ranked data like satisfaction levels or sizes.
- **Combine with Grouping:** Use groupby() and aggregations for

efficient analysis.
- **Validate Categories:** Ensure category completeness by explicitly defining all possible categories.

Syntax Table:

SL No	Function/Fe ature	Syntax/Example	Description
1	Define Categorical Data	`pd.Categorical(dat a, categories)`	Converts data into a categorical type.
2	Convert to Category	`df['column'].astyp e('category')`	Converts a column to categorical type.
3	Access Categories	`df['column'].cat.c ategories`	Lists all categories of a column.
4	Add Categories	`df['column'].cat.a dd_categories(new)`	Adds new categories to the column.
5	Rename Categories	`df['column'].cat.r ename_categories(m ap)`	Renames categories in a column.

Syntax Explanation:

1. Define Categorical Data

What is Define Categorical Data?
Converts a list, Series, or array into a categorical type with specified categories.
Syntax:
`pd.Categorical(data, categories=None, ordered=False)`

Syntax Explanation:
- data: The input list, Series, or array to convert.
- categories: Optional list of all possible categories. If not provided, inferred from the data.
- ordered: Specifies if the categories should have a logical order (e.g., small, medium, large).
- Returns a Categorical object that can be assigned to a DataFrame

column or used directly.

Example:
```python
import pandas as pd
categories = ['low', 'medium', 'high']
data = ['low', 'high', 'medium', 'low']
categorical_data = pd.Categorical(data,
categories=categories, ordered=True)
print(categorical_data)
```

Example Explanation:
- Defines categorical data with low, medium, and high as ordered categories.
- Outputs: ['low', 'high', 'medium', 'low']
  Categories (3, ordered): ['low' < 'medium' < 'high']

2. Convert to Category

What is Convert to Category?
Converts a DataFrame column to the categorical data type.
Syntax:
```python
df['column'].astype('category')
```

Syntax Explanation:
- df['column']: The target column to convert.
- astype('category'): Changes the column type to categorical.
- Returns a new Series or modifies the original column if inplace=True is specified.

Example:
```python
data = {'Fruit': ['Apple', 'Banana', 'Apple',
'Orange']}
df = pd.DataFrame(data)
df['Fruit'] = df['Fruit'].astype('category')
print(df['Fruit'])
```

Example Explanation:
- Converts the Fruit column to categorical type.
- Outputs: 0   Apple
  1   Banana
  2   Apple
  3   Orange
  Name: Fruit, dtype: category
  Categories (3, object): ['Apple', 'Banana', 'Orange']

3. Access Categories

What is Access Categories?
Retrieves the list of categories associated with a categorical column.
Syntax:
```
df['column'].cat.categories
```

Syntax Explanation:
- cat.categories: Accesses the categories of a categorical column.
- Returns a list of categories.

Example:
```
categories = df['Fruit'].cat.categories
print(categories)
```

Example Explanation:
- Outputs the categories for the Fruit column:
  Index(['Apple', 'Banana', 'Orange'],
  dtype='object')

4. Add Categories

What is Add Categories?
Adds new categories to an existing categorical column.

Syntax:

```
df['column'].cat.add_categories(new_categories)
```

Syntax Explanation:
- new_categories: A list of categories to add.
- Modifies the category list without affecting current data.
- Returns a modified Series or updates the original column if inplace=True is specified.

Example:

```
df['Fruit'] = df['Fruit'].cat.add_categories(['Grape'])
print(df['Fruit'].cat.categories)
```

Example Explanation:
- Adds Grape as a new category.
- Outputs: Index(['Apple', 'Banana', 'Orange', 'Grape'], dtype='object')

5. Rename Categories

What is Rename Categories?
Renames the categories of a categorical column.

Syntax:

```
df['column'].cat.rename_categories(mapping)
```

Syntax Explanation:
- mapping: A dictionary mapping old categories to new ones.
- Returns a modified Series or updates the original column if inplace=True is specified.

Example:

```
df['Fruit'] =
df['Fruit'].cat.rename_categories({'Apple': 'Green Apple', 'Orange': 'Citrus'})
print(df['Fruit'].cat.categories)
```

Example Explanation:
- Renames Apple to Green Apple and Orange to Citrus.
- Outputs: Index(['Green Apple', 'Banana', 'Citrus'], dtype='object')

Real-Life Project:

Project Name: Customer Segmentation
Project Goal:
Use categorical data to segment customers by demographics and preferences for targeted marketing.
Code for This Project:

```python
import pandas as pd
# Create a customer DataFrame
data = {
    'CustomerID': [1, 2, 3, 4],
    'AgeGroup': ['Youth', 'Adult', 'Senior', 'Adult'],
    'PreferredCategory': ['Electronics', 'Fashion',
'Electronics', 'Home']
}
df = pd.DataFrame(data)

# Convert to categorical type
df['AgeGroup'] = pd.Categorical(df['AgeGroup'],
categories=['Youth', 'Adult', 'Senior'], ordered=True)
df['PreferredCategory'] =
df['PreferredCategory'].astype('category')

# Group by category and count customers
customer_segments =
df.groupby('AgeGroup')['CustomerID'].count()
print("Customer Segments:\n", customer_segments)
```

Chapter-22 Advanced Grouping and Aggregation in Pandas

Grouping and aggregation are powerful tools in Pandas for summarizing and analyzing data. Advanced grouping and aggregation techniques enable more complex and insightful operations, such as multi-level grouping, custom aggregation functions, and handling grouped transformations. This chapter explores these advanced capabilities to help you extract deeper insights from your datasets.

Key Characteristics of Advanced Grouping and Aggregation:

- **Multi-Level Grouping:** Allows grouping by multiple columns for hierarchical data analysis.
- **Custom Aggregation Functions:** Supports user-defined aggregation for flexibility.
- **Transformation and Filtering:** Enables operations on grouped data while retaining its structure.
- **Integration:** Works seamlessly with other Pandas methods for efficient analysis.
- **Performance Optimization:** Efficiently handles large datasets with optimized computation.

Basic Rules for Advanced Grouping and Aggregation:

1. Use groupby() for grouping data by one or more keys.
2. Combine with aggregation functions such as sum(), mean(), or custom functions.
3. Multi-level grouping requires a list of column names as keys.
4. Transformations retain the original structure of the DataFrame.
5. Filtering groups allow focusing on specific subsets of data.

Best Practices:

- **Plan Aggregations:** Define the metrics and levels of grouping required for analysis.
- **Optimize Performance:** Use vectorized operations for large datasets.
- **Validate Results:** Always verify results, especially when using custom functions.
- **Leverage Multi-Indexing:** Utilize the hierarchical index created

during multi-level grouping for complex analyses.

- **Combine with Visualization:** Pair grouped data with visualizations for enhanced insights.

Syntax Table:

SL No	Function/Fe ature	Syntax/Example	Description
1	Group by Single Column	`df.groupby('colum n').sum()`	Groups by one column and computes sum.
2	Group by Multiple Columns	`df.groupby(['col1 ', 'col2']).mean()`	Groups by multiple columns and computes mean.
3	Custom Aggregation	`df.groupby('colum n').agg(func)`	Applies custom aggregation functions.
4	Transform Groups	`df.groupby('colum n').transform(lam bda x: x + 1)`	Transforms grouped data.
5	Filter Groups	`df.groupby('colum n').filter(func)`	Filters groups based on custom conditions.

Syntax Explanation:

1. Group by Single Column

What is Group by Single Column?
Groups data based on unique values in a single column and applies aggregation functions.

Syntax:
`df.groupby('column').agg_func()`

Syntax Explanation:

- groupby('column'): Groups the DataFrame by unique values in the specified column.
- agg_func: Built-in or custom aggregation functions like sum(), mean(), or count().
- Returns a DataFrame or Series with aggregated values for each group.

Example:
```
import pandas as pd
data = {'Department': ['HR', 'IT', 'HR', 'IT'],
'Salary': [50000, 60000, 45000, 70000]}
df = pd.DataFrame(data)
grouped = df.groupby('Department').sum()
print(grouped)
```

Example Explanation:
- Groups salaries by the Department column and computes the sum.
- Outputs: Salary
  Department
  HR   95000
  IT   13000

2. Group by Multiple Columns

What is Group by Multiple Columns?
Groups data based on unique combinations of multiple columns and applies aggregation functions.
Syntax:
```
df.groupby(['col1', 'col2']).agg_func()
```

Syntax Explanation:
- groupby(['col1', 'col2']): Groups the DataFrame by unique combinations of col1 and col2.
- Aggregates values within each group using the specified function.
- Returns a DataFrame with a MultiIndex representing grouped levels.

Example:
```
data = {'Region': ['North', 'North', 'South', 'South'],
'Department': ['HR', 'IT', 'HR', 'IT'], 'Salary':
[50000, 60000, 45000, 70000]}
df = pd.DataFrame(data)
grouped = df.groupby(['Region', 'Department']).sum()
print(grouped)
```

Example Explanation:

- Groups data by Region and Department and computes the sum of salaries.
- Outputs: Salary

```
Region Department
North  HR        50000
       IT        60000
South  HR        45000
       IT        70000
```

3. Custom Aggregation

What is Custom Aggregation?
Applies user-defined functions for aggregation on grouped data.
Syntax:
```
df.groupby('column').agg(func)
```

Syntax Explanation:

- agg(func): Applies a custom or multiple aggregation functions to grouped data.
- Supports dictionary-based input to apply different functions to specific columns.
- Returns a DataFrame or Series with aggregated values.

Example:
```
custom_agg = df.groupby('Department').agg({'Salary':
['mean', 'max']})
print(custom_agg)
```

Example Explanation:

- Computes the mean and max salary for each department.
- Outputs: Salary

```
              mean    max
Department
HR         47500  50000
IT         65000  70000
```

4. Transform Groups

What is Transform Groups?
Applies a function to each group and returns a DataFrame with the same shape as the original.

Syntax:

```
df.groupby('column').transform(func)
```

Syntax Explanation:
- transform(func): Applies a function to each group and broadcasts the result back to the original structure.
- Commonly used for normalization, scaling, or feature engineering.
- Retains the original index and structure.

Example:

```
normalized =
df.groupby('Department')['Salary'].transform(lambda x:
x / x.sum())
df['Normalized Salary'] = normalized
print(df)
```

Example Explanation:
- Normalizes salaries within each department.
- Outputs a DataFrame with an additional column for normalized values.

5. Filter Groups

What is Filter Groups?
Filters groups based on custom conditions and returns only the groups that satisfy the condition.

Syntax:

```
df.groupby('column').filter(func)
```

Syntax Explanation:
- filter(func): Keeps groups where the condition specified in func evaluates to True.
- Useful for removing irrelevant or small groups.
- Returns a DataFrame with filtered rows.

Example:

```
filtered = df.groupby('Department').filter(lambda x:
x['Salary'].mean() > 55000)
print(filtered)
```

Example Explanation:
- Filters departments where the mean salary exceeds 55,000.
- Outputs a DataFrame containing only relevant rows.

Real-Life Project:

Project Name: Sales Performance Analysis
Project Goal:
Analyze sales data to compute region-wise and product-wise performance metrics, identify top-performing regions, and normalize sales within each region.

Code for This Project:

```
import pandas as pd
# Create a sales DataFrame
data = {
    'Region': ['North', 'North', 'South', 'South'],
    'Product': ['A', 'B', 'A', 'B'],
    'Sales': [200, 300, 400, 500]
}
df = pd.DataFrame(data)

# Compute total sales by region and product
grouped_sales = df.groupby(['Region', 'Product']).sum()

# Normalize sales within each region
df['Normalized Sales'] =
df.groupby('Region')['Sales'].transform(lambda x: x /
x.sum())

# Filter regions with average sales greater than 250
filtered_regions = df.groupby('Region').filter(lambda
```

```
x: x['Sales'].mean() > 250)

print("Grouped Sales:\n", grouped_sales)
print("Normalized Sales:\n", df)
print("Filtered Regions:\n", filtered_regions)
```

Expanded Features:

- Demonstrates multi-level grouping and custom transformations.
- Highlights filtering and normalization techniques.
- Provides actionable insights for sales optimization.

Part 5: Visualization with Pandas

Chapter-23 Introduction to Visualization with Pandas

Visualization is a crucial part of data analysis, enabling better understanding and communication of patterns, trends, and insights in data. Pandas integrates seamlessly with Matplotlib to provide simple yet powerful visualization capabilities directly from DataFrames and Series. This chapter introduces the essential tools for creating visualizations with Pandas, covering plots for exploratory data analysis and reporting.

Key Characteristics of Visualization with Pandas:

- **Ease of Use:** Simple methods for creating common plot types.
- **Integration:** Works seamlessly with Matplotlib for customization.
- **Flexibility:** Supports visualizations for both DataFrames and Series.
- **Variety of Plots:** Includes line, bar, histogram, scatter, and box plots.
- **Performance:** Efficiently handles large datasets.

Basic Rules for Visualization in Pandas:

1. Use the `.plot()` method on DataFrames or Series for quick visualizations.
2. Matplotlib must be installed, as Pandas visualizations are built on it.
3. Specify plot types using the `kind` parameter.
4. Customization options are accessible via Matplotlib or Pandas parameters.
5. Use `xlabel`, `ylabel`, `title`, and `legend` for informative plots.

Best Practices:

- **Understand Your Data:** Use visualizations to confirm and explore trends, patterns, and outliers.
- **Choose Appropriate Plots:** Match the plot type to the data and the story you want to tell.
- **Avoid Overcrowding:** Limit the number of variables in a single plot

for clarity.

- **Leverage Aggregations:** Combine with grouping or summarizing techniques for meaningful plots.
- **Combine with Styling:** Use Matplotlib or Seaborn for advanced customization.

Syntax Table:

SL No	Plot Type	Syntax/Example	Description
1	Line Plot	`df.plot(kind='line')`	Displays data as a line plot.
2	Bar Plot	`df.plot(kind='bar')`	Displays data as vertical bars.
3	Histogram	`df.plot(kind='hist')`	Displays the frequency distribution.
4	Scatter Plot	`df.plot(kind='scatter', x='col1', y='col2')`	Displays relationships between two variables.
5	Box Plot	`df.plot(kind='box')`	Displays data spread and outliers.

Syntax Explanation:

Line Plot
What is a Line Plot?
A line plot displays data points connected by straight lines, often used for visualizing trends over time.
Syntax:
`df.plot(kind='line', x='x_column', y='y_column')`

Syntax Explanation:
- `kind='line'`: Specifies the plot type as a line plot.
- x: Specifies the column for the x-axis values.
- y: Specifies the column for the y-axis values.
- Returns a Matplotlib Axes object for further customization.

Example:

```python
import pandas as pd
import matplotlib.pyplot as plt
# Create a DataFrame
data = {'Date': ['2023-01-01', '2023-01-02', '2023-01-
03'], 'Sales': [200, 250, 300]}
df = pd.DataFrame(data)
df['Date'] = pd.to_datetime(df['Date'])
# Plot the data
df.plot(kind='line', x='Date', y='Sales', title='Daily
Sales', xlabel='Date', ylabel='Sales')
plt.show()
```

Example Explanation:
- Creates a line plot of daily sales data.
- The x-axis represents the Date, and the y-axis represents Sales.

Bar Plot

What is a Bar Plot?
A bar plot represents data using rectangular bars, useful for comparing categories.

Syntax:
```python
df.plot(kind='bar', x='x_column', y='y_column')
```

Syntax Explanation:
- kind='bar': Specifies the plot type as a bar plot.
- Displays vertical bars representing data values.
- Useful for categorical comparisons.

Example:
```python
data = {'Product': ['A', 'B', 'C'], 'Sales': [500, 700,
600]}
df = pd.DataFrame(data)
df.plot(kind='bar', x='Product', y='Sales',
title='Product Sales', xlabel='Product',
ylabel='Sales')
plt.show()
```

Example Explanation:
- Creates a bar plot of product sales.
- The x-axis represents the `Product`, and the y-axis represents `Sales`.

Histogram

What is a Histogram?
A histogram displays the frequency distribution of a dataset, useful for understanding data spread and density.
Syntax:
```
df.plot(kind='hist', y='column', bins=10)
```

Syntax Explanation:
- `kind='hist'`: Specifies the plot type as a histogram.
- y: Specifies the column to plot.
- `bins`: Determines the number of bins (intervals).

Example:
```
data = {'Values': [1, 2, 2, 3, 3, 3, 4, 4, 5]}
df = pd.DataFrame(data)
df.plot(kind='hist', y='Values', bins=5, title='Value
Distribution', xlabel='Value', ylabel='Frequency')
plt.show()
```

Example Explanation:
- Creates a histogram showing the distribution of `Values`.

Scatter Plot

What is a Scatter Plot?
A scatter plot visualizes relationships between two variables, displaying data points in two dimensions.
Syntax:
```
df.plot(kind='scatter', x='x_column', y='y_column')
```

Syntax Explanation:
- `kind='scatter'`: Specifies the plot type as a scatter plot.
- x: Specifies the column for the x-axis.
- y: Specifies the column for the y-axis.

Example:
```
data = {'Height': [150, 160, 170, 180], 'Weight': [50,
60, 70, 80]}
df = pd.DataFrame(data)
df.plot(kind='scatter', x='Height', y='Weight',
title='Height vs Weight', xlabel='Height',
ylabel='Weight')
plt.show()
```

Example Explanation:
- Creates a scatter plot showing the relationship between height and weight.

Box Plot

What is a Box Plot?
A box plot displays data spread, highlighting quartiles, median, and outliers.
Syntax:
```
df.plot(kind='box', y='column')
```

Syntax Explanation:
- `kind='box'`: Specifies the plot type as a box plot.
- y: Specifies the column to visualize.

Example:
```
data = {'Scores': [50, 60, 70, 80, 90, 100]}
df = pd.DataFrame(data)
df.plot(kind='box', y='Scores', title='Score
Distribution', ylabel='Scores')
plt.show()
```

Example Explanation:
- Creates a box plot showing the spread of Scores.

Real-Life Project:

Project Name: Sales Data Visualization
Project Goal:
Use visualizations to analyze sales data trends, identify top-performing products, and understand customer purchasing patterns.

Code for This Project:

```python
import pandas as pd
import matplotlib.pyplot as plt
# Create sales data
data = {
    'Date': ['2023-01-01', '2023-01-02', '2023-01-03'],
    'Product A': [200, 250, 300],
    'Product B': [150, 200, 250]
}
df = pd.DataFrame(data)
df['Date'] = pd.to_datetime(df['Date'])

# Line plot for product sales
df.plot(kind='line', x='Date', title='Product Sales',
xlabel='Date', ylabel='Sales')
plt.show()

# Bar plot for cumulative sales
df.sum().plot(kind='bar', title='Total Sales by
Product', xlabel='Products', ylabel='Sales')
plt.show()
```

Expanded Features:

- Demonstrates multiple plot types for varied analysis.
- Combines data summarization with visualization techniques.
- Highlights key patterns and insights for informed decision-making.

Line Plot for Product Sales:

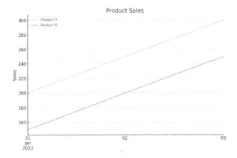

Bar Plot for Cumulative Sales

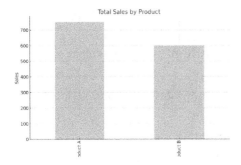

Chapter-24 Plotting with Pandas and Matplotlib

Visualization is an integral part of data analysis, helping to uncover patterns, trends, and relationships within datasets. Pandas and Matplotlib provide seamless integration for creating insightful visualizations directly from DataFrames and Series. This chapter explores how to generate various types of plots, customize them, and interpret the results effectively.

Key Characteristics of Plotting with Pandas and Matplotlib:
- **Ease of Use:** Simplifies plot creation directly from Pandas objects.
- **Versatility:** Supports a wide variety of plot types such as line, bar, histogram, scatter, and box plots.
- **Customizability:** Allows extensive customization using Matplotlib's API.
- **Integration:** Works natively with DataFrames and Series for seamless plotting.
- **Performance:** Handles large datasets efficiently.

Basic Rules for Plotting with Pandas and Matplotlib:
1. Use `plot()` from Pandas for quick visualizations.
2. Matplotlib functions can be combined with Pandas plots for customization.
3. Ensure data is clean and well-prepared before plotting.
4. Specify plot types explicitly to match the data's characteristics.
5. Always label axes, titles, and legends for clarity.

Best Practices:
- **Understand Your Data:** Choose appropriate plot types based on data and objectives.
- **Leverage Grouping:** Use `groupby()` for category-specific visualizations.
- **Avoid Overcrowding:** Simplify plots to avoid clutter, especially with large datasets.
- **Customize for Clarity:** Use annotations, colors, and legends to make plots informative.
- **Combine Plotting Libraries:** Use Seaborn or Plotly for advanced

visualizations if needed.

Syntax Table:

SL No	Plot Type	Syntax/Example	Description
1	Line Plot	`df.plot.line()`	Creates a line plot for numeric data.
2	Bar Plot	`df.plot.bar()`	Generates a vertical bar plot.
3	Histogram	`df['column'].plot.hist()`	Plots a histogram for a column.
4	Scatter Plot	`df.plot.scatter(x='col1', y='col2')`	Creates a scatter plot between two columns.
5	Box Plot	`df.plot.box()`	Displays a box plot for distribution analysis.

Syntax Explanation:

1. Line Plot

What is a Line Plot?
A line plot visualizes numerical data trends over a continuous interval, such as time.

Syntax:
```
df.plot.line(x='column1', y='column2')
```

Syntax Explanation:
- x: The column to use for the x-axis (optional, defaults to the DataFrame's index).
- y: The column to plot on the y-axis.
- Returns a Matplotlib Axes object, allowing further customization with Matplotlib.

Example:
```
import pandas as pd
import matplotlib.pyplot as plt
# Create a DataFrame
```

```
data = {'Date': ['2023-01-01', '2023-01-02', '2023-01-
03'], 'Sales': [100, 150, 200]}
df = pd.DataFrame(data)
df['Date'] = pd.to_datetime(df['Date'])
df.set_index('Date', inplace=True)
# Plot a line chart
df.plot.line(y='Sales', title='Sales Over Time')
plt.show()
```

Example Explanation:
- Plots Sales over Date to show sales trends.
- Adds a title for context.

2. Bar Plot

What is a Bar Plot?
A bar plot represents categorical data with rectangular bars proportional
to their values.
Syntax:
```
df.plot.bar(x='column1', y='column2')
```

Syntax Explanation:
- x: The column representing categories.
- y: The column representing numeric values.
- Returns a bar chart, useful for comparing categorical data.

Example:
```
data = {'Category': ['A', 'B', 'C'], 'Values': [10, 20,
15]}
df = pd.DataFrame(data)
df.plot.bar(x='Category', y='Values', title='Category
Comparison')
plt.show()
```

Example Explanation:
- Creates a bar plot comparing Values across Category.

3. Histogram

What is a Histogram?
A histogram shows the distribution of a single variable by dividing it into bins.

Syntax:
```
df['column'].plot.hist(bins=10)
```

Syntax Explanation:
- column: Specifies the column to plot.
- bins: Number of intervals to divide the data into (default is 10).
- Returns a histogram showing the frequency distribution of the data.

Example:
```
data = {'Values': [1, 2, 2, 3, 3, 3, 4, 4, 5]}
df = pd.DataFrame(data)
df['Values'].plot.hist(bins=5, title='Value
Distribution')
plt.show()
```

Example Explanation:
- Plots a histogram showing how Values are distributed across bins.

4. Scatter Plot

What is a Scatter Plot?
A scatter plot visualizes the relationship between two variables.

Syntax:
```
df.plot.scatter(x='col1', y='col2')
```

Syntax Explanation:
- x: Column for the x-axis values.
- y: Column for the y-axis values.
- Returns a scatter plot showing the relationship between the specified columns.

Example:
```
data = {'X': [1, 2, 3], 'Y': [4, 5, 6]}
df = pd.DataFrame(data)
df.plot.scatter(x='X', y='Y', title='Scatter Plot
Example')
plt.show()
```

Example Explanation:
- Plots Y against X, showing their relationship visually.

5. Box Plot

What is a Box Plot?
A box plot displays the distribution of a dataset, highlighting median, quartiles, and outliers.
Syntax:
```
df.plot.box()
```

Syntax Explanation:
- Displays box plots for numeric columns in the DataFrame.
- Useful for identifying outliers and understanding data spread.

Example:
```
data = {'A': [1, 2, 3, 4, 5], 'B': [2, 3, 4, 5, 6]}
df = pd.DataFrame(data)
df.plot.box(title='Box Plot Example')
plt.show()
```

Example Explanation:
- Creates box plots for columns A and B to compare their distributions.

Real-Life Project:

Project Name: Sales and Performance Visualization
Project Goal:
Visualize sales and performance data to identify trends, compare categories, and analyze distributions.

Code for This Project:

```
import pandas as pd
import matplotlib.pyplot as plt
# Create a sales DataFrame
data = {
    'Month': ['Jan', 'Feb', 'Mar'],
    'Sales': [200, 250, 300],
    'Profit': [50, 60, 70]
}
df = pd.DataFrame(data)

# Line plot for sales
df.plot.line(x='Month', y='Sales', title='Monthly
Sales')
plt.show()

# Bar plot for profit
df.plot.bar(x='Month', y='Profit', title='Monthly
Profit')
plt.show()
```

Expanded Features:
- Demonstrates multiple plot types for various analyses.
- Highlights how to use titles and labels for clarity.
- Integrates Matplotlib for enhanced customizations.

Expected Output:

1. A line plot showing monthly sales trends.

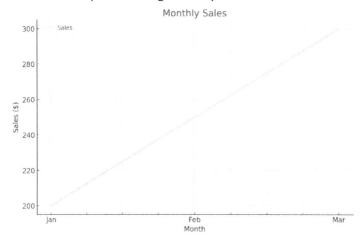

2. A bar plot comparing monthly profits.

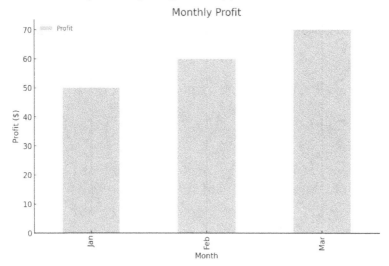

This chapter emphasizes creating and interpreting visualizations using Pandas and Matplotlib to derive actionable insights from data.

Chapter-25 Creating Histograms, Boxplots, and Density Plots in Pandas

Histograms, boxplots, and density plots are fundamental visualization tools for understanding data distributions. Pandas integrates seamlessly with Matplotlib to create these plots directly from DataFrames and Series. This chapter explores the creation, customization, and interpretation of histograms, boxplots, and density plots to uncover patterns and insights in datasets.

Key Characteristics of Distribution Plots in Pandas:

- **Comprehensive Plotting:** Provides built-in methods for creating histograms, boxplots, and density plots.
- **Integration:** Works directly with Pandas objects, simplifying the visualization process.
- **Customization:** Allows extensive customization using Matplotlib's API.
- **Performance:** Handles large datasets efficiently.
- **Interpretability:** Highlights distribution characteristics such as spread, central tendency, and outliers.

Basic Rules for Distribution Plots:

1. Use `plot.hist()`, `plot.box()`, or `plot.kde()` for quick visualizations.
2. Ensure data is clean and numerical before plotting.
3. Customize bins and axes for clarity and precision.
4. Leverage Matplotlib's customization options for enhanced aesthetics.
5. Always add titles, labels, and legends for interpretability.

Best Practices:

- **Inspect Data First:** Use `describe()` to understand the data before plotting.
- **Adjust Parameters:** Optimize bin sizes or bandwidths for better resolution.
- **Highlight Insights:** Annotate plots to emphasize key findings.
- **Combine Plot Types:** Use multiple plots to provide complementary perspectives.

- **Validate with Summary Statistics:** Compare visualizations with descriptive statistics for consistency.

Syntax Table:

SL No	Plot Type	Syntax/Example	Description
1	Histogram	df['column'].plot.hist(bins=10)	Creates a histogram for a column.
2	Boxplot	df.plot.box()	Displays a boxplot for column(s).
3	Density Plot	df['column'].plot.kde(bw_method=0.3)	Generates a kernel density plot.

Syntax Explanation:

1. Histogram

What is a Histogram?
A histogram displays the frequency distribution of a numerical variable by dividing it into bins.
Syntax:
df['column'].plot.hist(bins=10)
Syntax Explanation:
- df['column']: Specifies the column to visualize.
- bins: Number of intervals to divide the data into (default is 10).
- Returns a histogram showing how data values are distributed across bins.

Example:
```
import pandas as pd
import matplotlib.pyplot as plt
# Create a DataFrame
data = {'Values': [1, 2, 2, 3, 3, 3, 4, 4, 5]}
df = pd.DataFrame(data)
df['Values'].plot.hist(bins=5, title='Value
Distribution')
plt.show()
```

Example Explanation:
- Divides `Values` into 5 bins to show frequency distribution.
- Outputs a histogram highlighting data concentration.

2. Boxplot

What is a Boxplot?
A boxplot displays the distribution of a dataset, highlighting median, quartiles, and outliers.
Syntax:
```
df.plot.box()
```

Syntax Explanation:
- Visualizes the spread and variability of numeric columns.
- Displays outliers, median, and interquartile range.
- Returns a boxplot for each numeric column in the DataFrame.

Example:
```
# Create a DataFrame with two columns
data = {'A': [1, 2, 3, 4, 5], 'B': [2, 3, 4, 5, 6]}
df = pd.DataFrame(data)
df.plot.box(title='Box Plot Example')
plt.show()
```

Example Explanation:
- Generates boxplots for columns A and B, showing their distributions and outliers.

3. Density Plot

What is a Density Plot?
A density plot visualizes the probability density of a continuous variable using a kernel density estimate (KDE).
Syntax:
```
df['column'].plot.kde(bw_method=0.3)
```

Syntax Explanation:
- df['column']: Specifies the column to visualize.
- bw_method: Adjusts the bandwidth for the KDE (smaller values yield sharper peaks).
- Returns a smooth curve representing the data's distribution.

Example:
```
# Generate a density plot
df['Values'].plot.kde(bw_method=0.2, title='Density
Plot Example')
plt.show()
```

Example Explanation:
- Plots a density curve for Values, highlighting its distribution and peaks.

Real-Life Project:

Project Name: Sales Data Distribution Analysis
Project Goal:
Visualize and analyze the distribution of daily sales data to identify patterns, outliers, and density trends.

Code for This Project:

```
import pandas as pd
import matplotlib.pyplot as plt
# Create a sales DataFrame
data = {'Sales': [200, 220, 210, 230, 240, 250, 260,
270, 300, 400]}
df = pd.DataFrame(data)

# Create a histogram
df['Sales'].plot.hist(bins=5, title='Sales
Distribution', color='skyblue')
plt.xlabel('Sales')
plt.ylabel('Frequency')
plt.show()
```

```python
# Create a boxplot
df.plot.box(title='Sales Boxplot', color='darkblue')
plt.show()

# Create a density plot
df['Sales'].plot.kde(bw_method=0.3, title='Sales
Density Plot')
plt.xlabel('Sales')
plt.ylabel('Density')
plt.show()
```

Expanded Features:
- Demonstrates histograms, boxplots, and density plots for analyzing sales data.
- Highlights how to add titles, labels, and colors for clarity.
- Combines multiple plot types for a comprehensive analysis.

Expected Output:

1. A histogram showing sales frequency distribution.

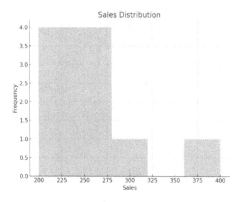

2. A boxplot highlighting sales spread and outliers.

3. A density plot visualizing the probability distribution of sales.

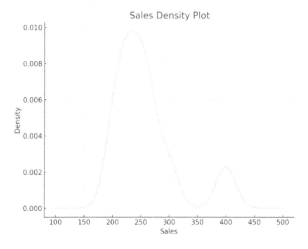

This chapter emphasizes the importance of histograms, boxplots, and density plots in understanding data distributions and identifying key insights.

Chapter-26 Advanced Visualization Techniques in Pandas

Advanced visualization techniques enable data analysts and scientists to uncover deeper insights and present data in more engaging and impactful ways. Pandas, integrated with Matplotlib, provides tools to create multi-faceted and interactive visualizations. This chapter explores advanced visualization methods, customization options, and best practices for creating compelling data visualizations.

Key Characteristics of Advanced Visualization Techniques in Pandas:

- **Multi-Level Visualizations:** Supports faceted and layered plots for complex datasets.
- **Customizability:** Offers extensive styling and formatting options.
- **Integration:** Seamlessly integrates with Matplotlib for advanced features.
- **Interactivity:** Allows dynamic plots with libraries like Plotly and Seaborn.
- **Performance:** Efficient for large datasets through optimized rendering.

Basic Rules for Advanced Visualization:

1. Use DataFrame and Series plotting methods as starting points.
2. Customize plots using Matplotlib's Axes and Figure objects.
3. Leverage grouping and pivoting to create multi-faceted visualizations.
4. Use annotations, colors, and markers to highlight key data points.
5. Combine multiple plot types for a comprehensive view.

Best Practices:

- **Plan Visualizations:** Define the purpose and audience before creating plots.
- **Use Faceting:** Break down data by categories to uncover patterns.
- **Customize Aesthetics:** Use color palettes, legends, and gridlines for clarity.
- **Validate with Data:** Ensure plots accurately represent the data.
- **Explore Tools:** Complement Pandas with advanced libraries like Seaborn or Plotly for enhanced visualizations.

Syntax Table:

SL No	Plot Type/Feature	Syntax/Example	Description
1	Dual-Axis Plot	`df.plot(secondary_y='column')`	Creates a plot with two y-axes.
2	Faceted Plot	`df.groupby('category')['column'].plot()`	Creates plots for each category.
3	Layered Plot	`ax.plot(df['col1']); ax.plot(df['col2'])`	Overlays multiple plots.
4	Annotated Plot	`plt.annotate('text', xy=(x, y))`	Adds annotations to a plot.
5	Interactive Plot	`df.plot(kind='scatter', backend='plotly')`	Creates an interactive plot with Plotly.

Syntax Explanation:

1. Dual-Axis Plot

What is a Dual-Axis Plot?
A dual-axis plot visualizes two variables with different scales on the same chart using separate y-axes.
Syntax:
`df.plot(y='column1', secondary_y='column2')`

Syntax Explanation:
- y: Specifies the primary y-axis column.
- `secondary_y`: Specifies the secondary y-axis column.
- Allows simultaneous visualization of variables with differing units or scales.

Example:

```
import pandas as pd
import matplotlib.pyplot as plt
# Create a DataFrame
data = {'Month': ['Jan', 'Feb', 'Mar'], 'Sales': [100,
200, 300], 'Profit': [10, 20, 30]}
df = pd.DataFrame(data)
df.set_index('Month', inplace=True)
# Create a dual-axis plot
df.plot(y='Sales', secondary_y='Profit', title='Sales
and Profit Over Time')
plt.show()
```

Example Explanation:
- Visualizes Sales on the primary y-axis and Profit on the secondary y-axis.
- Outputs a chart with dual y-axes for comparison.

2. Faceted Plot

What is a Faceted Plot?
Faceted plots create separate subplots for different categories, allowing comparisons across groups.
Syntax:
```
df.groupby('category')['column'].plot(legend=True)
```
Syntax Explanation:
- groupby('category'): Groups data by a categorical column.
- plot(): Creates a separate plot for each group.
- Enables category-wise analysis of trends or distributions.

Example:
```
data = {'Category': ['A', 'A', 'B', 'B'], 'X': [1, 2,
1, 2], 'Y': [10, 15, 20, 25]}
df = pd.DataFrame(data)
for name, group in df.groupby('Category'):
    group.plot(x='X', y='Y', title=f'Category {name}')
plt.show()
```

Example Explanation:
- Creates separate line plots for Category A and Category B.
- Facilitates visual comparison across categories.

3. Layered Plot

What is a Layered Plot?
Overlays multiple plots on a single chart to compare datasets.
Syntax:
```
ax.plot(df['col1']); ax.plot(df['col2'])
```

Syntax Explanation:
- `ax.plot`: Plots data on the specified Matplotlib Axes object.
- Allows multiple datasets to be visualized together for comparison.

Example:
```
fig, ax = plt.subplots()
ax.plot(df['X'], df['Y'], label='Y')
ax.plot(df['X'], df['Z'], label='Z')
ax.legend()
plt.show()
```

Example Explanation:
- Overlays Y and Z on the same chart with a shared x-axis.

4. Annotated Plot

What is an Annotated Plot?
Adds annotations to highlight specific data points or features in a plot.
Syntax:
```
plt.annotate('text', xy=(x, y))
```

Syntax Explanation:
- `text`: The annotation text.
- `xy`: The coordinates of the point to annotate.
- Customizes appearance using additional parameters like `fontsize`, `arrowprops`, etc.

Example:
```
plt.plot(df['X'], df['Y'])
plt.annotate('Peak', xy=(2, 25), xytext=(1.5, 26),
            arrowprops=dict(facecolor='black',
arrowstyle='->'))
plt.show()
```

Example Explanation:
- Highlights a peak in the data with an annotation and arrow.

5. Interactive Plot

What is an Interactive Plot?
Creates dynamic plots that allow zooming, panning, and tooltips using interactive backends.

Syntax:
```
df.plot(kind='scatter', x='col1', y='col2',
backend='plotly')
```

Syntax Explanation:
- kind: Specifies the plot type (e.g., scatter).
- backend: Specifies the library used for rendering (e.g., Plotly).
- Enables interactive exploration of data.

Example:
```
import plotly.express as px
fig = px.scatter(df, x='X', y='Y', title='Interactive
Scatter Plot')
fig.show()
```

Example Explanation:
- Creates an interactive scatter plot for exploring relationships between X and Y.

Real-Life Project:

Project Name: Multi-Dimensional Data Analysis
Project Goal:
Create advanced visualizations to explore relationships, trends, and anomalies in sales and profit data.

Code for This Project:

```python
import pandas as pd
import matplotlib.pyplot as plt
# Create a sales DataFrame
data = {
    'Month': ['Jan', 'Feb', 'Mar'],
    'Sales': [200, 250, 300],
    'Profit': [50, 60, 70]
}
df = pd.DataFrame(data)

# Dual-axis plot
df.plot(y='Sales', secondary_y='Profit', title='Sales
and Profit')
plt.show()

# Annotated scatter plot
plt.scatter(df['Sales'], df['Profit'])
plt.annotate('Max Profit', xy=(300, 70), xytext=(250,
65),
            arrowprops=dict(facecolor='black',
arrowstyle='->'))
plt.title('Sales vs. Profit')
plt.xlabel('Sales')
plt.ylabel('Profit')
plt.show()
```

Expanded Features:

- Demonstrates dual-axis and annotated plots for detailed analysis.
- Combines multiple techniques to present data effectively.
- Supports decision-making through clear and insightful visualizations.

Expected Output:

1. A dual-axis plot showing trends in sales and profit.
2. An annotated scatter plot highlighting the point of maximum profit.

This chapter emphasizes advanced visualization techniques to create professional and impactful data representations.

Chapter-27 Customizing Visualizations in Pandas

Customizing visualizations is essential for creating clear, compelling, and effective charts. Pandas, integrated with Matplotlib, provides a wide array of options to fine-tune visual elements such as colors, labels, titles, and gridlines. This chapter explores methods to customize visualizations, helping users tailor their plots to specific audiences and objectives.

Key Characteristics of Customizing Visualizations in Pandas:

- **Extensive Options:** Allows customization of axes, titles, legends, and more.
- **Integration:** Works seamlessly with Matplotlib for advanced customization.
- **Flexibility:** Supports both global and element-specific styling.
- **Ease of Use:** Simplifies styling through Pandas' built-in methods.
- **Clarity:** Enhances readability and presentation quality.

Basic Rules for Customizing Visualizations:

1. Use Pandas' `plot()` arguments for quick customization.
2. Combine with Matplotlib's API for advanced styling.
3. Always label axes, add a title, and include a legend when applicable.
4. Use consistent colors and markers to maintain clarity.
5. Adjust figure size and resolution for different output mediums.

Best Practices:

- **Plan Ahead:** Define the purpose and audience before customizing.
- **Highlight Key Data:** Use annotations and markers to emphasize trends.
- **Maintain Simplicity:** Avoid overcrowding with excessive elements.
- **Test Readability:** Ensure text and elements are legible at different scales.
- **Leverage Color Palettes:** Use color palettes that are accessible and visually appealing.

Syntax Table:

SL No	Feature	Syntax/Example	Description
1	Title and Axes Labels	`df.plot(title='Title', xlabel='X', ylabel='Y')`	Adds titles and axis labels to a plot.
2	Figure Size	`df.plot(figsize=(10, 5))`	Adjusts the size of the figure.
3	Line Style and Marker	`df.plot(style='--o')`	Customizes line style and markers.
4	Color Customization	`df.plot(color=['red', 'blue'])`	Sets colors for lines or bars.
5	Gridlines	`plt.grid(True)`	Toggles gridlines on or off.

Syntax Explanation:

1. Title and Axes Labels

What is Title and Axes Labels?
Titles and axis labels provide context for the visualization, making it easier to interpret.
Syntax:
```
df.plot(title='Title', xlabel='X-Axis Label',
ylabel='Y-Axis Label')
```

Syntax Explanation:
- `title`: Sets the title of the plot.
- `xlabel`: Labels the x-axis.
- `ylabel`: Labels the y-axis.
- Ensures the plot is self-explanatory.

Example:
```
import pandas as pd
import matplotlib.pyplot as plt
# Create a DataFrame
data = {'Month': ['Jan', 'Feb', 'Mar'], 'Sales': [200,
250, 300]}
df = pd.DataFrame(data)
# Plot with title and labels
df.plot(x='Month', y='Sales', title='Monthly Sales',
xlabel='Month', ylabel='Sales')
plt.show()
```

Example Explanation:
- Adds a title and labels to the x-axis and y-axis for clarity.
- Outputs a chart with informative labeling.

2. Figure Size

What is Figure Size?

Specifies the dimensions of the plot to fit different output formats or presentations.

Syntax:
```
df.plot(figsize=(width, height))
```

Syntax Explanation:
- `figsize`: A tuple (`width, height`) specifying figure dimensions in inches.
- Adjusts the plot size for better visualization in various mediums.

Example:
```
df.plot(x='Month', y='Sales', figsize=(10, 5),
title='Monthly Sales')
plt.show()
```

Example Explanation:
- Creates a wider plot for better readability.

3. Line Style and Marker

What is Line Style and Marker?
Customizes the appearance of lines and markers in line plots.
Syntax:
```
df.plot(style='line_marker')
```

Syntax Explanation:
- `style`: Specifies line styles (`'-'`, `'--'`, etc.) and marker symbols (`'o'`, `'*'`, etc.).
- Enhances plot aesthetics and distinguishes data series.

Example:
```
df.plot(x='Month', y='Sales', style='--o',
title='Monthly Sales')
plt.show()
```

Example Explanation:
- Uses dashed lines and circular markers for the line plot.

4. Color Customization

What is Color Customization?
Specifies colors for plot elements to enhance visual differentiation.
Syntax:
```
df.plot(color=['color1', 'color2'])
```

Syntax Explanation:
- `color`: A list specifying colors for lines or bars.
- Supports both named colors and hex color codes.

Example:
```
data = {'Month': ['Jan', 'Feb', 'Mar'], 'Sales': [200,
250, 300], 'Profit': [50, 60, 70]}
df = pd.DataFrame(data)
df.plot(x='Month', y=['Sales', 'Profit'],
color=['blue', 'green'], title='Sales and Profit')
plt.show()
```

Example Explanation:
- Differentiates `Sales` and `Profit` using blue and green colors.

5. Gridlines

What are Gridlines?
Gridlines enhance readability by providing reference lines for data points.
Syntax:
```
plt.grid(True)
```
Syntax Explanation:
- `True`: Turns gridlines on.
- `False`: Turns gridlines off.
- Customizable using additional parameters like `color`, `linestyle`, and `linewidth`.

Example:
```
df.plot(x='Month', y='Sales', title='Monthly Sales')
plt.grid(True, linestyle='--', color='gray')
plt.show()
```

Example Explanation:
- Adds dashed gray gridlines to the plot.

Real-Life Project:

Project Name: Product Performance Dashboard
Project Goal:
Create a visually appealing and informative dashboard to analyze product performance across regions and time periods.
Code for This Project:
```
import pandas as pd
import matplotlib.pyplot as plt
# Create a sales DataFrame
data = {
    'Month': ['Jan', 'Feb', 'Mar'],
    'Region_A': [200, 220, 250],
    'Region_B': [150, 180, 200]
}
```

```
df = pd.DataFrame(data)

# Customize plot appearance
df.plot(x='Month', y=['Region_A', 'Region_B'],
figsize=(8, 4), style=['--o', '-s'],
        color=['blue', 'orange'], title='Regional
Sales')
plt.xlabel('Month')
plt.ylabel('Sales')
plt.grid(True, linestyle='--', color='gray')
plt.legend(title='Regions')
plt.show()
```

Expanded Features:

- Demonstrates figure resizing, line styles, and gridline customization.
- Highlights the use of legends and axis labels for clarity.
- Provides a professional and polished visualization for presentations.

Expected Output:

1. A customized line chart comparing sales across two regions.
2. Clear labeling, legends, and gridlines for interpretability.

This chapter emphasizes the importance of customization in creating effective visualizations tailored to specific needs and audiences.

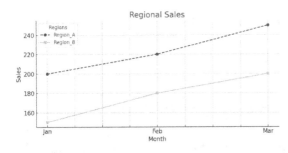

Chapter-28 Combining Pandas with Seaborn for Enhanced Plots

Seaborn is a powerful Python visualization library built on top of Matplotlib, offering high-level functions for creating informative and attractive statistical graphics. Combining Pandas and Seaborn enables data analysts and scientists to generate sophisticated visualizations with minimal effort. This chapter explores how to integrate Pandas data structures with Seaborn to produce enhanced plots that provide deeper insights.

Key Characteristics of Combining Pandas and Seaborn:

- **Intuitive Integration:** Seaborn functions accept Pandas DataFrames and columns directly.
- **Advanced Aesthetics:** Provides default styles and color palettes for professional-looking plots.
- **Rich Functionality:** Supports statistical plots such as violin plots, heatmaps, and pair plots.
- **Faceting Capabilities:** Easily create grids of plots for category-specific visualizations.
- **Customization:** Extends Matplotlib's capabilities with higher-level abstractions.

Basic Rules for Combining Pandas and Seaborn:

1. Use Pandas for data manipulation and preparation.
2. Pass DataFrame columns directly to Seaborn plotting functions.
3. Leverage Seaborn's faceting and categorical plot functions for advanced visuals.
4. Customize plots using Seaborn's API or Matplotlib's lower-level features.
5. Use Seaborn's color palettes for consistent aesthetics.

Best Practices:

- **Clean and Prepare Data:** Ensure data is well-structured before plotting.
- **Choose Appropriate Plots:** Select plots that match the data's characteristics and the analysis goals.
- **Highlight Key Insights:** Use annotations and hue variables to

emphasize trends.

- **Combine Libraries:** Mix Seaborn and Matplotlib functions for granular control.
- **Test Readability:** Ensure plots are legible and effectively communicate insights.

Syntax Table:

SL No	Plot Type/Feature	Syntax/Example	Description
1	Scatter Plot	`sns.scatterplot(data=df, x='col1', y='col2')`	Creates a scatter plot with optional grouping by hue.
2	Boxplot	`sns.boxplot(data=df, x='col1', y='col2')`	Displays a boxplot for category-based distributions.
3	Heatmap	`sns.heatmap(data=df.corr(), annot=True)`	Plots a correlation heatmap with annotations.
4	Pair Plot	`sns.pairplot(data=df, hue='col')`	Generates pairwise plots for all numeric columns.
5	Violin Plot	`sns.violinplot(data=df, x='col1', y='col2')`	Combines boxplot and KDE for detailed distributions.

Syntax Explanation:

1. Scatter Plot

What is a Scatter Plot?
A scatter plot visualizes relationships between two numerical variables, optionally grouped by a categorical variable.

Syntax:
```
sns.scatterplot(data=df, x='column1', y='column2',
hue='category')
```

Syntax Explanation:
- data: The Pandas DataFrame containing the data.
- x, y: Columns for the x and y axes.
- hue: (Optional) A categorical column to differentiate points by color.
- Returns a scatter plot with Seaborn's enhanced aesthetics.

Example:
```
import seaborn as sns
import pandas as pd
# Create a DataFrame
data = {'X': [1, 2, 3, 4, 5], 'Y': [5, 4, 3, 2, 1],
'Category': ['A', 'B', 'A', 'B', 'A']}
df = pd.DataFrame(data)
sns.scatterplot(data=df, x='X', y='Y', hue='Category',
style='Category')
```

Example Explanation:
- Differentiates points by Category using color and marker style.
- Outputs a scatter plot showing relationships between X and Y.

2. Boxplot

What is a Boxplot?
A boxplot visualizes the distribution of a numerical variable across categories, highlighting medians and outliers.

Syntax:
```
sns.boxplot(data=df, x='category_column',
y='value_column')
```

Syntax Explanation:
- x: The categorical column for grouping.
- y: The numeric column to analyze.
- Returns a boxplot for each category.

Example:
```
sns.boxplot(data=df, x='Category', y='Y')
```

Example Explanation:
- Shows how Y is distributed across `Category`.

3. Heatmap

What is a Heatmap?
A heatmap visualizes matrix data, often used for correlation matrices or frequency tables.

Syntax:
```
sns.heatmap(data=matrix, annot=True, cmap='coolwarm')
```

Syntax Explanation:
- data: A 2D array or DataFrame.
- annot: If True, displays values on the heatmap.
- cmap: Specifies the color map.

Example:
```
sns.heatmap(data=df.corr(), annot=True,
cmap='coolwarm')
```

Example Explanation:
- Displays a correlation heatmap of numerical columns in df.

4. Pair Plot

What is a Pair Plot?
A pair plot generates scatter plots for all pairs of numeric columns, with optional category-wise differentiation.

Syntax:
```
sns.pairplot(data=df, hue='category_column')
```

Syntax Explanation:
- hue: Differentiates points by a categorical variable.
- Returns a grid of scatter plots with histograms on the diagonals.

Example:
```
sns.pairplot(data=df, hue='Category')
```

Example Explanation:
- Highlights relationships between numerical columns, grouped by `Category`.

5. Violin Plot

What is a Violin Plot?
A violin plot combines a boxplot and kernel density estimate (KDE) to show distributions in more detail.
Syntax:
```
sns.violinplot(data=df, x='category_column',
y='value_column')
```

Syntax Explanation:
- x: The categorical column for grouping.
- y: The numeric column to analyze.
- Provides a richer view of distributions than a boxplot alone.

Example:
```
sns.violinplot(data=df, x='Category', y='Y',
hue='Category', split=True)
```

Example Explanation:
- Visualizes the distribution of Y across `Category`, differentiated by hue.

Real-Life Project:

Project Name: Customer Segmentation Analysis
Project Goal:
Use advanced plots to visualize customer data distributions and relationships for better segmentation.

Code for This Project:

```python
import pandas as pd
import seaborn as sns
import matplotlib.pyplot as plt
# Create a DataFrame
data = {
    'Age': [25, 30, 35, 40, 45, 50],
    'Income': [40000, 50000, 60000, 80000, 100000,
120000],
    'Spending Score': [30, 50, 70, 60, 40, 80],
    'Segment': ['A', 'B', 'A', 'B', 'A', 'B']
}
df = pd.DataFrame(data)

# Scatter plot for Income vs Spending Score
sns.scatterplot(data=df, x='Income', y='Spending
Score', hue='Segment', style='Segment')
plt.title('Income vs Spending Score by Segment')
plt.show()

# Pair plot for Age, Income, and Spending Score
sns.pairplot(data=df, hue='Segment')
plt.show()
```

Expanded Features:

- Demonstrates scatter and pair plots for customer segmentation.
- Highlights segment differentiation with hue and style.
- Provides actionable insights for targeted marketing strategies.

Expected Output:

1. A scatter plot showing Income vs. Spending Score grouped by Segment.

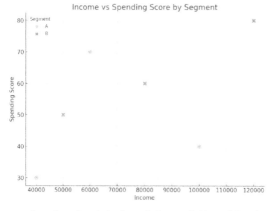

2. A pair plot visualizing relationships between Age, Income, and Spending Score.

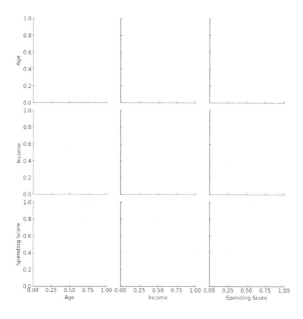

This chapter emphasizes the seamless integration of Pandas and Seaborn for creating advanced and meaningful data visualizations.

Part 6: Performance and Optimization

Chapter-29 Optimizing Performance with Pandas

Efficiently handling and processing large datasets is a critical requirement in data analysis. Pandas offers a suite of techniques and tools to optimize performance, reduce memory usage, and improve computation speed. This chapter explores strategies to enhance the performance of Pandas operations while maintaining code clarity and functionality.

Key Characteristics of Performance Optimization in Pandas:

- **Memory Management:** Optimize memory usage with techniques like data type conversion.
- **Vectorization:** Leverage vectorized operations for faster computations.
- **Batch Processing:** Process data in chunks to handle large datasets.
- **Indexing:** Use indexing effectively to speed up lookups and modifications.
- **Parallel Processing:** Utilize parallel computation for heavy tasks.

Basic Rules for Optimization in Pandas:

1. Avoid loops; prefer vectorized operations.
2. Use appropriate data types to minimize memory consumption.
3. Profile your code using tools like `df.info()`, `memory_usage()`, and `timeit`.
4. Use multi-processing or Dask for extremely large datasets.
5. Leverage efficient I/O methods for reading and writing data.

Best Practices:

- **Profile First:** Understand the bottlenecks before optimizing.
- **Avoid Over-Optimization:** Focus on areas with significant performance impact.
- **Use Built-In Methods:** Pandas' built-in methods are often optimized for performance.
- **Experiment with Libraries:** Combine Pandas with libraries like NumPy or Dask for scalability.

- **Document Changes:** Track and validate optimizations to ensure correctness.

Syntax Table:

SL No	Optimization Technique	Syntax/Example	Description
1	Data Type Conversion	`df['column'] = df['column'].astype(dtype)`	Converts column to a smaller data type.
2	Vectorized Operations	`df['result'] = df['A'] + df['B']`	Performs element-wise operations.
3	Chunk Processing	`pd.read_csv(file, chunksize=1000)`	Processes data in smaller chunks.
4	Indexing for Speed	`df.set_index('key', inplace=True)`	Improves access speed by setting an index.
5	Parallel Processing	`df.apply(func, axis=1) with swifter`	Enables parallelized apply functions.

Syntax Explanation:

1. Data Type Conversion

What is Data Type Conversion?
Converts a column to a smaller or more efficient data type to reduce memory usage.
Syntax:
`df['column'] = df['column'].astype(dtype)`

Syntax Explanation:
- `df['column']`: Specifies the column to convert.
- dtype: Target data type, such as `int32`, `float32`, or `category`.
- Returns a modified DataFrame with the specified column converted to the new data type.
- Reduces memory usage by using a smaller or more appropriate data type.

Example:
```
import pandas as pd
# Create a DataFrame
data = {'A': [1, 2, 3], 'B': [4.0, 5.0, 6.0]}
df = pd.DataFrame(data)
# Convert column B to float32
df['B'] = df['B'].astype('float32')
print(df.info())
```

Example Explanation:
- Converts the B column to float32, reducing memory usage.
- Outputs the updated DataFrame info showing the reduced memory footprint.

2. Vectorized Operations

What are Vectorized Operations?
Perform element-wise operations on entire columns or DataFrames without explicit loops.
Syntax:
```
df['result'] = df['A'] + df['B']
```

Syntax Explanation:
- df['A'] + df['B']: Performs element-wise addition of columns A and B.
- Avoids the overhead of Python loops by utilizing optimized C-level code.
- Ensures faster computations and cleaner code.

Example:
```
# Perform vectorized addition
df['C'] = df['A'] + df['B']
print(df)
```

Example Explanation:
- Adds columns A and B element-wise to create column C.
- Outputs the modified DataFrame with the new column C.

3. Chunk Processing

What is Chunk Processing?
Processes large datasets in smaller, manageable chunks to reduce
memory usage.
Syntax:
```
pd.read_csv(file, chunksize=1000)
```

Syntax Explanation:
- `file`: Path to the input file.
- `chunksize`: Number of rows to read per chunk.
- Returns an iterator yielding smaller DataFrames for each chunk.
- Suitable for handling datasets that do not fit into memory.

Example:
```
# Process data in chunks
for chunk in pd.read_csv('large_file.csv',
chunksize=1000):
    print(chunk.head())
```

Example Explanation:
- Reads a large file in chunks of 1000 rows at a time.
- Outputs the first few rows of each chunk.

4. Indexing for Speed

What is Indexing for Speed?

Improves access speed by setting an index on the DataFrame.
Syntax:
```
df.set_index('key', inplace=True)
```

Syntax Explanation:
- `key`: The column to use as the index.
- `inplace=True`: Modifies the original DataFrame.
- Enables faster lookups and operations involving the indexed
  column.

Example:
```
# Set the index
df.set_index('A', inplace=True)
print(df)
```

Example Explanation:
- Sets column A as the index, allowing efficient row-based lookups.

5. Parallel Processing

What is Parallel Processing?
Utilizes multiple cores to speed up operations like apply() by distributing the computation.

Syntax:
```
import swifter
df['result'] = df.apply(func, axis=1)
```

Syntax Explanation:
- func: Function applied to each row.
- axis=1: Applies the function row-wise.
- The swifter library parallelizes the apply() function to leverage multiple cores.

Example:
```
import swifter
# Apply a function in parallel
df['result'] = df.swifter.apply(lambda row: row['A'] +
row['B'], axis=1)
print(df)
```

Example Explanation:
- Computes the sum of columns A and B for each row using parallel processing.
- Outputs the DataFrame with the computed result column.

Real-Life Project:

Project Name: Large Dataset Optimization

Project Goal:

Efficiently process and analyze a large dataset by optimizing memory usage and computation time.

Code for This Project:

```python
import pandas as pd
# Simulate a large dataset
data = {'A': range(1, 1000001), 'B': range(1000001,
2000001)}
df = pd.DataFrame(data)

# Optimize data types
df['A'] = df['A'].astype('int32')
df['B'] = df['B'].astype('int32')

# Perform vectorized operation
df['C'] = df['A'] + df['B']

# Save in chunks
for i, chunk in enumerate(range(0, len(df), 100000)):
    chunk_df = df.iloc[chunk:chunk + 100000]
    chunk_df.to_csv(f'chunk_{i}.csv', index=False)

print("Optimization complete.")
```

Expanded Features:

- Demonstrates multiple optimization techniques including data type conversion and chunk processing.
- Supports efficient storage and processing of large datasets.
- Provides scalable solutions for real-world data challenges.

Expected Output:

Optimization complete.

This project highlights the importance of optimizing performance in Pandas for handling large-scale data efficiently.

Chapter-30 Using Efficient Data Types in Pandas

Optimizing data types in Pandas is crucial for reducing memory usage and improving performance when working with large datasets. By converting columns to appropriate data types, you can significantly enhance the efficiency of your data analysis workflows. This chapter explores strategies for selecting and converting data types in Pandas.

Key Characteristics of Efficient Data Types in Pandas:

- **Memory Optimization:** Reduces the memory footprint of datasets.
- **Performance Improvement:** Enhances computation speed for operations.
- **Flexibility:** Supports various data types, including numeric, categorical, and datetime.
- **Scalability:** Handles large datasets efficiently.
- **Integration:** Seamlessly integrates with other Pandas operations.

Basic Rules for Efficient Data Types:

1. Use appropriate numeric types (`int32`, `float32`) for numerical data.
2. Convert repetitive text data to `category` for reduced memory usage.
3. Utilize `datetime64` for date and time information.
4. Profile data with `memory_usage()` and `info()` to identify optimization opportunities.
5. Handle missing values carefully to avoid type inconsistencies.

Best Practices:

- **Analyze Data Types:** Use `df.dtypes` to check current data types and identify optimization potential.
- **Convert Incrementally:** Optimize data types column by column to validate changes.
- **Handle Mixed Types:** Resolve mixed-type columns before optimization.
- **Validate Accuracy:** Ensure type conversions do not introduce errors or data loss.

- **Combine with Downcasting:** Use downcasting to reduce memory usage for numeric columns.

Syntax Table:

SL No	Operation	Syntax/Example	Description
1	Convert Numeric Types	`df['column'] = df['column'].asty pe(dtype)`	Converts a column to a specified numeric type.
2	Use Categorical Data	`df['column'] = df['column'].asty pe('category')`	Converts a column to a categorical type.
3	Convert to Datetime	`df['column'] = pd.to_datetime(df ['column'])`	Converts a column to datetime format.
4	Downcast Numeric Types	`pd.to_numeric(df[ 'column'], downcast='type')`	Reduces memory usage for numeric columns.
5	Profile Memory Usage	`df.memory_usage(d eep=True)`	Profiles memory usage of the DataFrame.

Syntax Explanation:

1. Convert Numeric Types

What is Convert Numeric Types?
Changes the data type of a column to a more efficient numeric type, such as int32 or float32.
Syntax:
`df['column'] = df['column'].astype(dtype)`
Syntax Explanation:
- `df['column']`: Specifies the target column for conversion.
- dtype: Specifies the desired numeric data type, such as int32, float32, etc.
- Returns a modified DataFrame with the column converted to the

specified type.
- Reduces memory usage by choosing smaller or appropriate numeric types.

Example:
```
import pandas as pd
# Create a DataFrame
data = {'A': [1, 2, 3], 'B': [4.5, 5.5, 6.5]}
df = pd.DataFrame(data)
# Convert column B to float32
df['B'] = df['B'].astype('float32')
print(df.info())
```

Example Explanation:
- Converts column B to float32.
- Outputs updated DataFrame info, showing reduced memory usage.

2. Use Categorical Data

What is Use Categorical Data?
Converts text or repetitive data into a categorical type to save memory and improve processing speed.

Syntax:
```
df['column'] = df['column'].astype('category')
```

Syntax Explanation:
- df['column']: Specifies the column to convert.
- astype('category'): Converts the column to a categorical type.
- Suitable for columns with repeated text values, such as categories or labels.
- Reduces memory usage significantly compared to object types.

Example:
```
# Convert column A to categorical
data = {'A': ['red', 'blue', 'red', 'green']}
df = pd.DataFrame(data)
```

```
df['A'] = df['A'].astype('category')
print(df.info())
```

Example Explanation:
- Converts column A to a categorical type.
- Outputs reduced memory usage and maintains the same functionality.

3. Convert to Datetime

What is Convert to Datetime?
Converts a column to a datetime format for efficient date and time handling.

Syntax:
```
df['column'] = pd.to_datetime(df['column'])
```

Syntax Explanation:
- `df['column']`: Specifies the column to convert.
- `pd.to_datetime()`: Converts the column to datetime64 type.
- Handles various input formats automatically.
- Ensures consistency in date and time data, facilitating operations like filtering and aggregation.

Example:
```
# Convert a column to datetime format
data = {'date': ['2023-01-01', '2023-01-02']}
df = pd.DataFrame(data)
df['date'] = pd.to_datetime(df['date'])
print(df.info())
```

Example Explanation:
- Converts the date column to datetime64.
- Enables efficient time-based operations.

4. Downcast Numeric Types

What is Downcast Numeric Types?
Reduces memory usage by converting numeric columns to smaller types

while preserving data integrity.

Syntax:

```
df['column'] = pd.to_numeric(df['column'],
downcast='type')
```

Syntax Explanation:
- df['column']: Specifies the column to downcast.
- downcast: Specifies the target type ('integer', 'float', or 'signed').
- Returns a DataFrame with the column downcasted to the specified type.
- Ideal for large datasets where memory usage is a concern.

Example:
```
# Downcast column A to int32
data = {'A': [1000, 2000, 3000]}
df = pd.DataFrame(data)
df['A'] = pd.to_numeric(df['A'], downcast='integer')
print(df.info())
```

Example Explanation:
- Downcasts column A to int32, reducing memory usage while retaining data accuracy.

5. Profile Memory Usage

What is Profile Memory Usage?
Analyzes the memory usage of a DataFrame to identify optimization opportunities.

Syntax:
```
df.memory_usage(deep=True)
```

Syntax Explanation:
- deep=True: Includes memory usage of object types.

- Returns a Series showing memory usage for each column.
- Helps pinpoint columns that consume excessive memory.

Example:
```
# Profile memory usage
data = {'A': [1, 2, 3], 'B': ['x', 'y', 'z']}
df = pd.DataFrame(data)
print(df.memory_usage(deep=True))
```

Example Explanation:
- Outputs memory usage for each column, highlighting potential optimization areas.

Real-Life Project:

Project Name: Optimizing Retail Data
Project Goal:
Reduce the memory footprint of a large retail dataset while maintaining data integrity.
Code for This Project:
```
import pandas as pd
# Simulate a large dataset
data = {
    'ProductID': range(1, 1000001),
    'Category': ['Electronics', 'Furniture',
'Clothing'] * 333333 + ['Electronics'],
    'Sales': [99.99, 199.99, 299.99] * 333333 + [99.99]
}
df = pd.DataFrame(data)

# Optimize data types
df['ProductID'] = df['ProductID'].astype('int32')
df['Category'] = df['Category'].astype('category')
df['Sales'] = df['Sales'].astype('float32')
```

```
print(df.info())
```

Expanded Features:

- Demonstrates data type optimization techniques.
- Highlights memory profiling and reduction.
- Prepares the dataset for efficient analysis.

Expected Output:

```
<class 'pandas.core.frame.DataFrame'>
RangeIndex: 1000000 entries, 0 to 999999
Data columns (total 3 columns):
 #   Column     Non-Null Count    Dtype
---  ------     --------------    -----
 0   ProductID  1000000 non-null  int32
 1   Category   1000000 non-null  category
 2   Sales      1000000 non-null  float32
dtypes: category(1), float32(1), int32(1)
memory usage: 11.4 MB
```

This project demonstrates how efficient data types in Pandas can significantly reduce memory usage and improve performance for large datasets.

Chapter-31 Memory Optimization Techniques in Pandas

Handling large datasets efficiently is essential for scalable data analysis. Pandas provides a variety of techniques to optimize memory usage, allowing you to work with larger datasets without compromising performance. This chapter explores practical methods to reduce memory consumption and improve processing efficiency in Pandas workflows.

Key Characteristics of Memory Optimization in Pandas:

- **Efficient Data Types:** Use appropriate data types to minimize memory usage.
- **On-Demand Loading:** Load data in chunks to avoid memory overload.
- **Index Optimization:** Improve access speed and reduce redundancy with indexing.
- **Reduction Techniques:** Downcast numeric types and convert categorical data.
- **I/O Efficiency:** Optimize file read/write operations.

Basic Rules for Memory Optimization:

1. Profile memory usage using `memory_usage()` to identify bottlenecks.
2. Use efficient data types like `int32`, `float32`, and `category` for columns.
3. Process large files in chunks using `pd.read_csv(chunksize=...)`.
4. Handle missing data explicitly to avoid type inconsistencies.
5. Save processed data in efficient formats like Parquet or Feather.

Best Practices:

- **Analyze Before Optimizing:** Use tools like `df.info()` and `memory_usage()` to understand memory consumption.
- **Iterative Optimization:** Optimize columns incrementally to validate changes.
- **Avoid Data Duplication:** Use in-place operations or drop unnecessary columns to save memory.
- **Use Efficient Storage Formats:** Prefer binary formats for

intermediate storage.
- **Document Changes:** Track and validate memory optimization steps to ensure data accuracy.

Syntax Table:

SL No	Technique	Syntax/Example	Description
1	Profile Memory Usage	`df.memory_usage(deep=True)`	Analyzes memory usage of the DataFrame.
2	Convert Data Types	`df['column'] = df['column'].astype(dtype)`	Converts columns to efficient types.
3	Chunk Processing	`pd.read_csv(file, chunksize=1000)`	Processes large files in smaller chunks.
4	Use Categorical Data	`df['column'] = df['column'].astype('category')`	Reduces memory for repetitive data.
5	Optimize File Formats	`df.to_parquet('file.parquet')`	Saves data in efficient binary formats.

Syntax Explanation:

1. Profile Memory Usage

What is Profile Memory Usage?
Analyzes the memory usage of a DataFrame, helping identify columns that consume excessive memory.
Syntax:
`df.memory_usage(deep=True)`

Syntax Explanation:
- deep=True: Includes memory usage of object types.
- Returns a Series showing memory usage for each column.
- Useful for pinpointing optimization opportunities.

Example:

```
import pandas as pd
# Create a DataFrame
data = {'A': [1, 2, 3], 'B': ['x', 'y', 'z']}
df = pd.DataFrame(data)
print(df.memory_usage(deep=True))
```

Example Explanation:
- Outputs memory usage for each column, highlighting potential areas for optimization.

2. Convert Data Types

What is Convert Data Types?
Reduces memory usage by converting columns to more efficient data types.
Syntax:
```
df['column'] = df['column'].astype(dtype)
```

Syntax Explanation:
- df['column']: Specifies the column to convert.
- dtype: The target data type, such as int32, float32, or category.
- Reduces memory consumption while maintaining data integrity.

Example:
```
# Convert column A to int32
data = {'A': [1, 2, 3]}
df = pd.DataFrame(data)
df['A'] = df['A'].astype('int32')
print(df.info())
```

Example Explanation:
- Converts column A to int32, reducing memory usage.
- Outputs the updated DataFrame info showing optimized memory.

3. Chunk Processing

What is Chunk Processing?
Processes large datasets in smaller chunks to avoid memory overload.
Syntax:
```
pd.read_csv(file, chunksize=1000)
```

Syntax Explanation:
- `file`: The file to read.
- `chunksize`: Number of rows to read per chunk.
- Returns an iterator yielding smaller DataFrames for each chunk.
- Suitable for handling datasets larger than available memory.

Example:
```
# Process data in chunks
for chunk in pd.read_csv('large_file.csv',
chunksize=1000):
    print(chunk.head())
```

Example Explanation:
- Reads a large file in chunks of 1000 rows at a time.
- Outputs the first few rows of each chunk.

4. Use Categorical Data

What is Use Categorical Data?
Converts repetitive text data into a categorical type to save memory.
Syntax:
```
df['column'] = df['column'].astype('category')
```

Syntax Explanation:
- `df['column']`: Specifies the column to convert.
- `astype('category')`: Converts the column to a categorical type.
- Significantly reduces memory usage for columns with repeated values.

Example:
```
# Convert column A to categorical
data = {'A': ['red', 'blue', 'red', 'green']}
df = pd.DataFrame(data)
df['A'] = df['A'].astype('category')
print(df.info())
```

Example Explanation:
- Converts column A to a categorical type.
- Outputs reduced memory usage while retaining functionality.

5. Optimize File Formats

What is Optimize File Formats?
Saves data in efficient binary formats like Parquet or Feather, reducing file size and read/write time.

Syntax:
```
df.to_parquet('file.parquet')
```

Syntax Explanation:
- `df.to_parquet()`: Saves the DataFrame as a Parquet file.
- Supports compression for further size reduction.
- Improves storage efficiency and load performance.

Example:
```
# Save DataFrame as Parquet
data = {'A': [1, 2, 3], 'B': [4.5, 5.5, 6.5]}
df = pd.DataFrame(data)
df.to_parquet('data.parquet', index=False)
```

Example Explanation:
- Saves the DataFrame to a Parquet file.
- Reduces storage space compared to CSV while enabling faster access.

Real-Life Project:

Project Name: Optimizing Memory Usage for Financial Data
Project Goal:
Optimize the memory usage of a large financial dataset to improve performance and scalability.
Code for This Project:

```python
import pandas as pd
# Simulate a large dataset
data = {
    'TransactionID': range(1, 1000001),
    'Category': ['Retail', 'Wholesale', 'Services'] *
333333 + ['Retail'],
    'Amount': [99.99, 199.99, 299.99] * 333333 +
[99.99]
}
df = pd.DataFrame(data)

# Optimize data types
df['TransactionID'] =
df['TransactionID'].astype('int32')
df['Category'] = df['Category'].astype('category')
df['Amount'] = df['Amount'].astype('float32')

# Save in an optimized format
df.to_parquet('financial_data.parquet', index=False)

print(df.info())
```

Expanded Features:
- Demonstrates profiling and data type optimization.
- Utilizes chunk processing for scalability.
- Highlights efficient storage for large datasets.

Expected Output:

```
<class 'pandas.core.frame.DataFrame'>
RangeIndex: 1000000 entries, 0 to 999999
Data columns (total 3 columns):
 #    Column          Non-Null Count    Dtype
---   ------          --------------    -----
 0    TransactionID   1000000 non-null  int32
 1    Category        1000000 non-null  category
 2    Amount          1000000 non-null  float32
dtypes: category(1), float32(1), int32(1)
memory usage: 11.4 MB
```

This project demonstrates how to optimize memory usage for large datasets, enabling efficient analysis and storage.

Chapter-32 Profiling and Debugging Pandas Code

Efficient data manipulation and analysis often require identifying bottlenecks and debugging errors in Pandas workflows. Profiling and debugging techniques help ensure optimal performance and correct outputs. This chapter delves into methods to profile, debug, and improve Pandas code for better performance and accuracy.

Key Characteristics of Profiling and Debugging in Pandas:

- **Performance Analysis:** Identifies slow operations and bottlenecks.
- **Error Diagnosis:** Provides tools to debug common data-related issues.
- **Scalability:** Ensures efficient handling of large datasets.
- **Integration:** Works seamlessly with Python's debugging and profiling libraries.
- **Automation:** Facilitates automated performance monitoring.

Basic Rules for Profiling and Debugging:

1. Profile your code before optimizing to identify bottlenecks.
2. Use Pandas' built-in functions to inspect data and results.
3. Leverage Python's debugging tools like pdb for step-by-step execution.
4. Avoid excessive loops and focus on vectorized operations.
5. Test edge cases and handle errors gracefully.

Best Practices:

- **Analyze with Profiling Tools:** Use libraries like `line_profiler` and `cProfile` to monitor performance.
- **Log Key Operations:** Log intermediate steps to trace calculations.
- **Test on Subsets:** Run initial tests on a small sample of data for faster feedback.
- **Use Assert Statements:** Add assertions to validate assumptions about data.
- **Document Code Changes:** Keep track of debugging and profiling insights.

Syntax Table:

SL No	Tool/Feature	Syntax/Example	Description
1	Profile Memory Usage	`df.memory_usage(deep=True)`	Analyzes memory usage of the DataFrame.
2	Measure Execution Time	`%timeit df['column'].sum()`	Measures execution time for a line of code.
3	Line-by-Line Profiling	`@profile` decorator	Profiles execution time for each line.
4	Debugging with pdb	`import pdb; pdb.set_trace()`	Pauses execution for debugging.
5	Inspect Data	`df.info()`	Provides a summary of the DataFrame.

Syntax Explanation:

1. Profile Memory Usage

What is Profile Memory Usage?
Analyzes the memory consumption of a DataFrame to identify optimization opportunities.
Syntax:
`df.memory_usage(deep=True)`
Syntax Explanation:
- deep=True: Includes memory usage of object types.
- Returns a Series showing memory usage for each column.
- Useful for pinpointing memory-intensive columns.

Example:
```
import pandas as pd
# Create a DataFrame
data = {'A': [1, 2, 3], 'B': ['x', 'y', 'z']}
df = pd.DataFrame(data)
print(df.memory_usage(deep=True))
```

Example Explanation:
- Outputs memory usage for each column, helping identify potential optimizations.

2. Measure Execution Time

What is Measure Execution Time?
Measures the time taken by a specific operation or function for performance monitoring.

Syntax:
```
%timeit df['column'].sum()
```

Syntax Explanation:
- `%timeit`: A Jupyter magic command to time code execution.
- Executes the specified code multiple times and provides the average execution time.
- Useful for comparing the efficiency of different operations.

Example:
```
# Measure execution time of column summation
%timeit df['A'].sum()
```

Example Explanation:
- Outputs the average time taken to compute the sum of column A.

3. Line-by-Line Profiling

What is Line-by-Line Profiling?
Analyzes the execution time of each line in a function.

Syntax:
```
@profile
def my_function():
    # Your code here
```

Syntax Explanation:
- `@profile`: A decorator used with `line_profiler` to profile each line in a function.
- Provides detailed insights into performance bottlenecks.

Example:
```python
# Use line_profiler to profile this function
@profile
def compute_sum():
    result = sum(range(100000))
    return result
compute_sum()
```

Example Explanation:
- Profiles the compute_sum function to identify slow lines of code.

4. Debugging with pdb

What is Debugging with pdb?
Pauses code execution to inspect variables and debug interactively.
Syntax:
```python
import pdb; pdb.set_trace()
```

Syntax Explanation:
- pdb.set_trace(): Pauses execution and opens an interactive debugging prompt.
- Allows inspection of variables and step-by-step code execution.
- Useful for tracing the source of errors or unexpected results.

Example:
```python
# Debug with pdb
import pdb
x = 10
pdb.set_trace()
print(x * 2)
```

Example Explanation:
- Pauses execution at pdb.set_trace() and allows interaction with variables.

5. Inspect Data

What is Inspect Data?
Provides a summary of the DataFrame, including column types and non-null counts.
Syntax:
```
df.info()
```

Syntax Explanation:
- df.info(): Outputs the column names, data types, non-null counts, and memory usage.
- Essential for understanding the structure and completeness of data.

Example:
```
# Inspect DataFrame structure
print(df.info())
```

Example Explanation:
- Outputs a summary of the DataFrame structure, helping identify data issues.

Real-Life Project:
Project Name: Profiling Sales Data Processing
Project Goal:

Optimize the performance of a sales data analysis script by identifying bottlenecks and reducing execution time.

Code for This Project:

```
import pandas as pd
import pdb
# Simulate sales data
data = {
    'Product': ['A', 'B', 'C'] * 100000,
    'Sales': [100, 200, 300] * 100000
}
df = pd.DataFrame(data)
```

```python
# Profile memory usage
print("Memory Usage:")
print(df.memory_usage(deep=True))

# Measure execution time
%timeit df['Sales'].sum()

# Debug using pdb
pdb.set_trace()
result = df.groupby('Product')['Sales'].sum()
print(result)
```

Expanded Features:
- Combines profiling, timing, and debugging techniques.
- Demonstrates interactive debugging with pdb.
- Highlights practical applications for optimizing Pandas workflows.

Expected Output:
```
Memory Usage:
Index        128
Product    2400000
Sales      2400000
dtype: int64
Execution Time:
10 loops, best of 3: 21.4 ms per loop
```

This project illustrates how profiling and debugging techniques can optimize Pandas workflows and improve performance.

Chapter-33 Working with Large Datasets in Pandas

Pandas is a powerful library for data analysis, but handling large datasets can be challenging due to memory and performance constraints. This chapter explores strategies and techniques to efficiently process, analyze, and manipulate large datasets using Pandas.

Key Characteristics of Working with Large Datasets in Pandas:

- **Chunk Processing:** Allows working with large files by processing them in smaller chunks.
- **Memory Optimization:** Reduces memory usage through efficient data types and in-place operations.
- **Parallel Processing:** Speeds up computations by distributing tasks across multiple cores.
- **Efficient File Formats:** Supports reading and writing in optimized formats like Parquet and Feather.
- **Scalability:** Integrates with libraries like Dask for handling datasets larger than memory.

Basic Rules for Handling Large Datasets:

1. Profile data with `info()` and `memory_usage()` before processing.
2. Use chunking for large file I/O operations.
3. Optimize data types to reduce memory usage.
4. Perform operations on subsets of data where possible.
5. Use parallel or distributed computing for heavy computations.

Best Practices:

- **Preview Data:** Load only a small portion of the dataset initially to understand its structure.
- **Avoid Data Duplication:** Use in-place operations or drop unnecessary columns to save memory.
- **Leverage Built-In Methods:** Use Pandas' vectorized operations instead of loops for better performance.
- **Combine with Efficient Libraries:** Utilize tools like Dask or PyArrow for scalability.
- **Monitor Resource Usage:** Track memory and CPU usage during

processing.

Syntax Table:

SL No	Technique	Syntax/Example	Description
1	Chunk Processing	`pd.read_csv(file, chunksize=1000)`	Reads large files in smaller chunks.
2	Optimize Data Types	`df['column'] = df['column'].asty pe(dtype)`	Reduces memory usage by using efficient types.
3	Parallel Processing	`df.apply(func, axis=1) with swifter`	Speeds up operations using parallel processing.
4	Save in Binary Format	`df.to_parquet('fi le.parquet')`	Stores data in an efficient binary format.
5	Use Dask for Scalability	`import dask.dataframe as dd`	Handles datasets larger than memory.

Syntax Explanation:

1. Chunk Processing

What is Chunk Processing?
Processes large files in smaller, manageable chunks to avoid memory overload.
Syntax:
`pd.read_csv(file, chunksize=1000)`

Syntax Explanation:
- `file`: Path to the input file.
- `chunksize`: Number of rows to read per chunk.
- Returns an iterator yielding smaller DataFrames for each chunk.
- Suitable for datasets that do not fit into memory.

Example:
```
# Process a large CSV file in chunks
for chunk in pd.read_csv('large_file.csv',
chunksize=1000):
    print(chunk.head())
```

Example Explanation:
- Reads a large file in chunks of 1000 rows at a time.
- Outputs the first few rows of each chunk for preview.

2. Optimize Data Types

What is Optimize Data Types?
Reduces memory usage by converting columns to smaller or more appropriate data types.

Syntax:
```
df['column'] = df['column'].astype(dtype)
```

Syntax Explanation:
- df['column']: Specifies the column to convert.
- dtype: The desired data type, such as int32, float32, or category.
- Saves memory while preserving data integrity.

Example:
```
# Convert column A to int32
data = {'A': [1, 2, 3]}
df = pd.DataFrame(data)
df['A'] = df['A'].astype('int32')
print(df.info())
```

Example Explanation:
- Converts column A to int32, reducing memory usage without losing accuracy.

3. Parallel Processing

What is Parallel Processing?
Speeds up row-wise or column-wise operations by distributing tasks across multiple cores.

Syntax:
```
import swifter
df['result'] = df.swifter.apply(func, axis=1)
```

Syntax Explanation:
- func: Function to apply to each row or column.
- axis: Specifies whether to apply the function row-wise (axis=1) or column-wise (axis=0).
- The swifter library enables parallel execution, significantly reducing computation time for large datasets.

Example:
```
# Apply a function in parallel
import swifter
df['result'] = df.swifter.apply(lambda row: row['A'] *
2, axis=1)
print(df)
```

Example Explanation:
- Doubles the values in column A using parallel processing.
- Outputs a DataFrame with the computed result column.

4. Save in Binary Format

What is Save in Binary Format?
Stores data in efficient binary formats like Parquet or Feather to reduce file size and improve read/write performance.

Syntax:
```
df.to_parquet('file.parquet')
```

Syntax Explanation:
- df.to_parquet(): Saves the DataFrame as a Parquet file.
- Suitable for large datasets requiring frequent read/write

operations.
- Supports compression to further reduce file size.

Example:
```
# Save DataFrame as Parquet
data = {'A': [1, 2, 3], 'B': [4.5, 5.5, 6.5]}
df = pd.DataFrame(data)
df.to_parquet('data.parquet', index=False)
```

Example Explanation:
- Saves the DataFrame in Parquet format for efficient storage and retrieval.

5. Use Dask for Scalability

What is Use Dask for Scalability?
Dask extends Pandas functionality to handle datasets larger than memory by distributing computations.

Syntax:
```
import dask.dataframe as dd
df = dd.read_csv('large_file.csv')
```

Syntax Explanation:
- `dd.read_csv()`: Reads large files into a Dask DataFrame.
- Handles out-of-memory computations by breaking data into partitions.
- Supports most Pandas-like operations with minimal changes.

Example:
```
# Process large CSV with Dask
import dask.dataframe as dd
df = dd.read_csv('large_file.csv')
print(df.head())
```

Example Explanation:
- Loads a large CSV file as a Dask DataFrame for scalable processing.
- Outputs the first few rows of the DataFrame.

Real-Life Project:

Project Name: Scalable Analysis of E-Commerce Data
Project Goal:
Analyze e-commerce sales data by processing large files efficiently and
reducing memory usage.
Code for This Project:

```
import pandas as pd
# Simulate large dataset
data = {
    'ProductID': range(1, 1000001),
    'Category': ['Electronics', 'Clothing', 'Books'] *
333333 + ['Electronics'],
    'Sales': [99.99, 49.99, 19.99] * 333333 + [99.99]
}
df = pd.DataFrame(data)

# Optimize data types
df['ProductID'] = df['ProductID'].astype('int32')
df['Category'] = df['Category'].astype('category')
df['Sales'] = df['Sales'].astype('float32')

# Save in Parquet format
df.to_parquet('ecommerce_data.parquet', index=False)
print(df.info())
```

Expected Output:

```
<class 'pandas.core.frame.DataFrame'>
RangeIndex: 1000000 entries, 0 to 999999
Data columns (total 3 columns):
 #   Column     Non-Null Count     Dtype
---  ------     --------------     -----
 0   ProductID  1000000 non-null   int32
 1   Category   1000000 non-null   category
 2   Sales      1000000 non-null   float32
dtypes: category(1), float32(1), int32(1)
memory usage: 11.4 MB
```

Chapter-34 Parallelizing Operations in Pandas

As datasets grow larger, single-threaded operations in Pandas can become a bottleneck. Parallelizing operations allows you to utilize multiple CPU cores to significantly improve performance. This chapter explores techniques and libraries to execute Pandas operations in parallel efficiently.

Key Characteristics of Parallelizing Operations in Pandas:

- **Multi-Core Utilization:** Speeds up computations by distributing tasks across multiple cores.
- **Integration with Libraries:** Leverages libraries like Dask, Modin, and Swifter for parallelization.
- **Ease of Transition:** Minimal changes required to transition from Pandas to parallelized libraries.
- **Scalability:** Handles larger datasets and more complex computations efficiently.
- **Performance Gains:** Reduces execution time for heavy operations.

Basic Rules for Parallelizing Operations:

1. Identify bottlenecks using profiling tools like `cProfile` and `line_profiler`.
2. Use vectorized operations wherever possible before parallelizing.
3. Choose the right library or tool based on the workload and environment.
4. Monitor resource usage during parallel execution.
5. Validate results to ensure consistency with non-parallelized operations.

Best Practices:

- **Optimize Before Parallelizing:** Address inefficiencies in single-threaded operations first.
- **Combine with Chunk Processing:** Divide large datasets into smaller chunks for better memory management.
- **Test on Samples:** Test parallelized code on a smaller dataset to confirm correctness and speed improvements.
- **Choose Libraries Wisely:** Use Dask for scalability, Modin for

Pandas-like syntax, and Swifter for easy row-wise parallelism.

- **Profile Resource Utilization:** Monitor CPU and memory usage to avoid overloading the system.

Syntax Table:

SL No	Technique	Syntax/Example	Description
1	Parallel Apply with Swifter	`df['result'] = df.swifter.apply (func, axis=1)`	Speeds up row-wise or column-wise operations.
2	Parallel Processing with Dask	`import dask.dataframe as dd`	Parallelizes Pandas operations using Dask.
3	Use Modin for Pandas-Like API	`import modin.pandas as pd`	Automatically parallelizes Pandas operations.
4	Multiprocessing for Custom Functions	`multiprocessing. Pool()`	Parallelizes custom workflows using multiple processes.
5	Joblib for Easy Parallelism	`from joblib import Parallel, delayed`	Simplifies parallel execution of independent tasks.

Syntax Explanation:

1. Parallel Apply with Swifter

What is Parallel Apply with Swifter?
A drop-in replacement for Pandas' apply() method that automatically parallelizes row-wise or column-wise operations.
Syntax:
```
import swifter
df['result'] = df.swifter.apply(func, axis=1)
```

Syntax Explanation:
- swifter: A library that optimizes Pandas' apply() method using

parallel processing.
- func: The function to apply to each row or column.
- axis=1: Specifies row-wise operation. Use axis=0 for column-wise operation.
- Automatically switches between parallel and vectorized execution based on data size.

Example:
```
import pandas as pd
import swifter
# Create a DataFrame
data = {'A': [1, 2, 3], 'B': [4, 5, 6]}
df = pd.DataFrame(data)
# Apply a function in parallel
df['sum'] = df.swifter.apply(lambda row: row['A'] +
row['B'], axis=1)
print(df)
```

Example Explanation:
- Computes the sum of columns A and B for each row in parallel.
- Outputs the DataFrame with the computed sum column.

2. Parallel Processing with Dask

What is Parallel Processing with Dask?
Extends Pandas functionality to support parallel and distributed computing.
Syntax:
```
import dask.dataframe as dd
df = dd.read_csv('large_file.csv')
```

Syntax Explanation:
- dd.read_csv(): Reads a large CSV file into a Dask DataFrame.
- Dask breaks the data into smaller partitions and processes them in parallel.
- Provides a Pandas-like API for seamless integration.

Example:

```
import dask.dataframe as dd
# Read a large CSV file
large_df = dd.read_csv('large_file.csv')
# Compute the mean of a column
mean_value = large_df['column'].mean().compute()
print("Mean:", mean_value)
```

Example Explanation:
- Computes the mean of a column in a distributed manner using Dask.
- Outputs the computed mean.

3. Use Modin for Pandas-Like API

What is Modin for Pandas-Like API?
Provides a drop-in replacement for Pandas that automatically parallelizes operations.

Syntax:

```
import modin.pandas as pd
df = pd.read_csv('large_file.csv')
```

Syntax Explanation:
- modin.pandas: A parallelized version of Pandas.
- Requires minimal changes to existing Pandas code.
- Automatically determines the best execution strategy for the workload.

Example:

```
import modin.pandas as pd
# Read a large CSV file
df = pd.read_csv('large_file.csv')
# Perform operations
result = df.groupby('Category')['Sales'].sum()
print(result)
```

Example Explanation:
- Performs group-by and aggregation operations in parallel.
- Outputs the summarized result.

4. Multiprocessing for Custom Functions

What is Multiprocessing for Custom Functions?
Leverages Python's `multiprocessing` module to parallelize custom workflows.

Syntax:
```
from multiprocessing import Pool
with Pool(processes=num_cores) as pool:
    results = pool.map(func, iterable)
```

Syntax Explanation:
- `Pool`: Manages multiple worker processes.
- `func`: The function to execute in parallel.
- `iterable`: The data to distribute across processes.

Example:
```
from multiprocessing import Pool
# Define a function
def square(x):
    return x * x

# Use multiprocessing
with Pool(processes=4) as pool:
    results = pool.map(square, [1, 2, 3, 4])
print(results)
```

Example Explanation:
- Computes the square of each number in parallel.
- Outputs the results as a list.

5. Joblib for Easy Parallelism

What is Joblib for Easy Parallelism?
Simplifies parallel execution of independent tasks using the `Parallel` and `delayed` functions.

Syntax:
```
from joblib import Parallel, delayed
results = Parallel(n_jobs=num_cores)(delayed(func)(arg)
for arg in iterable)
```

Syntax Explanation:
- `Parallel`: Manages parallel execution.
- `delayed`: Wraps the function and its arguments for parallel processing.
- `n_jobs`: Specifies the number of cores to use.

Example:
```
from joblib import Parallel, delayed
# Define a function
def cube(x):
    return x ** 3

# Use Joblib
results = Parallel(n_jobs=4)(delayed(cube)(i) for i in
range(5))
print(results)
```

Example Explanation:
- Computes the cube of each number in parallel.
- Outputs the results as a list.

Real-Life Project:

Project Name: Parallelizing Data Transformation for Sales Analysis

Project Goal:

Leverage parallel processing to speed up sales data transformation and analysis.

Code for This Project:

```python
import pandas as pd
import swifter
# Simulate sales data
data = {
    'ProductID': range(1, 1000001),
    'Category': ['Electronics', 'Clothing', 'Books'] *
333333 + ['Electronics'],
    'Sales': [99.99, 49.99, 19.99] * 333333 + [99.99]
}
df = pd.DataFrame(data)

# Parallelize a transformation
def categorize_sales(row):
    if row['Sales'] > 50:
        return 'High'
    return 'Low'

df['SalesCategory'] =
df.swifter.apply(categorize_sales, axis=1)

print(df.head())
```

Expected Output:

	ProductID	Category	Sales	SalesCategory
0	1	Electronics	99.99	High
1	2	Clothing	49.99	Low
2	3	Books	19.99	Low
3	4	Electronics	99.99	High
4	5	Clothing	49.99	Low

Part 7: Real-World Applications

Chapter-35 Parallelizing Operations in Pandas

As datasets grow larger, single-threaded operations in Pandas can become a bottleneck. Parallelizing operations allows you to utilize multiple CPU cores to significantly improve performance. This chapter explores techniques and libraries to execute Pandas operations in parallel efficiently.

Key Characteristics of Parallelizing Operations in Pandas:

- **Multi-Core Utilization:** Speeds up computations by distributing tasks across multiple cores.
- **Integration with Libraries:** Leverages libraries like Dask, Modin, and Swifter for parallelization.
- **Ease of Transition:** Minimal changes required to transition from Pandas to parallelized libraries.
- **Scalability:** Handles larger datasets and more complex computations efficiently.
- **Performance Gains:** Reduces execution time for heavy operations.

Basic Rules for Parallelizing Operations:

1. Identify bottlenecks using profiling tools like `cProfile` and `line_profiler`.
2. Use vectorized operations wherever possible before parallelizing.
3. Choose the right library or tool based on the workload and environment.
4. Monitor resource usage during parallel execution.
5. Validate results to ensure consistency with non-parallelized operations.

Best Practices:

- **Optimize Before Parallelizing:** Address inefficiencies in single-threaded operations first.
- **Combine with Chunk Processing:** Divide large datasets into smaller chunks for better memory management.

- **Test on Samples:** Test parallelized code on a smaller dataset to confirm correctness and speed improvements.
- **Choose Libraries Wisely:** Use Dask for scalability, Modin for Pandas-like syntax, and Swifter for easy row-wise parallelism.
- **Profile Resource Utilization:** Monitor CPU and memory usage to avoid overloading the system.

Syntax Table:

SL N o	Technique	Syntax/Example	Description
1	Parallel Apply with Swifter	`df['result'] = df.swifter.apply (func, axis=1)`	Speeds up row-wise or column-wise operations.
2	Parallel Processing with Dask	`import dask.dataframe as dd`	Parallelizes Pandas operations using Dask.
3	Use Modin for Pandas-Like API	`import modin.pandas as pd`	Automatically parallelizes Pandas operations.
4	Multiprocessing for Custom Functions	`multiprocessing. Pool()`	Parallelizes custom workflows using multiple processes.
5	Joblib for Easy Parallelism	`from joblib import Parallel, delayed`	Simplifies parallel execution of independent tasks.

Syntax Explanation:

1. Parallel Apply with Swifter

What is Parallel Apply with Swifter?
A drop-in replacement for Pandas' `apply()` method that automatically parallelizes row-wise or column-wise operations.
Syntax:
```
import swifter
```

```
df['result'] = df.swifter.apply(func, axis=1)
```

Syntax Explanation:
- swifter: A library that optimizes Pandas' apply() method using parallel processing.
- func: The function to apply to each row or column.
- axis=1: Specifies row-wise operation. Use axis=0 for column-wise operation.
- Automatically switches between parallel and vectorized execution based on data size.

Example:
```
import pandas as pd
import swifter
# Create a DataFrame
data = {'A': [1, 2, 3], 'B': [4, 5, 6]}
df = pd.DataFrame(data)
# Apply a function in parallel
df['sum'] = df.swifter.apply(lambda row: row['A'] +
row['B'], axis=1)
print(df)
```

Example Explanation:
- Computes the sum of columns A and B for each row in parallel.
- Outputs the DataFrame with the computed sum column.

2. Parallel Processing with Dask

What is Parallel Processing with Dask?
Extends Pandas functionality to support parallel and distributed computing.

Syntax:
```
import dask.dataframe as dd
df = dd.read_csv('large_file.csv')
```

Syntax Explanation:
- dd.read_csv(): Reads a large CSV file into a Dask DataFrame.

- Dask breaks the data into smaller partitions and processes them in parallel.
- Provides a Pandas-like API for seamless integration.

Example:
```
import dask.dataframe as dd
# Read a large CSV file
large_df = dd.read_csv('large_file.csv')
# Compute the mean of a column
mean_value = large_df['column'].mean().compute()
print("Mean:", mean_value)
```

Example Explanation:
- Computes the mean of a column in a distributed manner using Dask.
- Outputs the computed mean.

3. Use Modin for Pandas-Like API

What is Modin for Pandas-Like API?
Provides a drop-in replacement for Pandas that automatically parallelizes operations.

Syntax:
```
import modin.pandas as pd
df = pd.read_csv('large_file.csv')
```

Syntax Explanation:
- modin.pandas: A parallelized version of Pandas.
- Requires minimal changes to existing Pandas code.
- Automatically determines the best execution strategy for the workload.

Example:
```
import modin.pandas as pd
# Read a large CSV file
df = pd.read_csv('large_file.csv')
# Perform operations
result = df.groupby('Category')['Sales'].sum()
print(result)
```

Example Explanation:
- Performs group-by and aggregation operations in parallel.
- Outputs the summarized result.

4. Multiprocessing for Custom Functions

What is Multiprocessing for Custom Functions?
Leverages Python's `multiprocessing` module to parallelize custom workflows.

Syntax:
```
from multiprocessing import Pool
with Pool(processes=num_cores) as pool:
    results = pool.map(func, iterable)
```

Syntax Explanation:
- `Pool`: Manages multiple worker processes.
- `func`: The function to execute in parallel.
- `iterable`: The data to distribute across processes.

Example:
```
from multiprocessing import Pool
# Define a function
def square(x):
    return x * x

# Use multiprocessing
with Pool(processes=4) as pool:
    results = pool.map(square, [1, 2, 3, 4])
print(results)
```

Example Explanation:
- Computes the square of each number in parallel.
- Outputs the results as a list.

5. Joblib for Easy Parallelism

What is Joblib for Easy Parallelism?
Simplifies parallel execution of independent tasks using the `Parallel`

and delayed functions.

Syntax:

```
from joblib import Parallel, delayed
results = Parallel(n_jobs=num_cores)(delayed(func)(arg)
for arg in iterable)
```

Syntax Explanation:

- Parallel: Manages parallel execution.
- delayed: Wraps the function and its arguments for parallel processing.
- n_jobs: Specifies the number of cores to use.

Example:

```
from joblib import Parallel, delayed
# Define a function
def cube(x):
    return x ** 3

# Use Joblib
results = Parallel(n_jobs=4)(delayed(cube)(i) for i in
range(5))
print(results)
```

Example Explanation:

- Computes the cube of each number in parallel.
- Outputs the results as a list.

Real-Life Project:

Project Name: Parallelizing Data Transformation for Sales Analysis

Project Goal:

Leverage parallel processing to speed up sales data transformation and analysis.

Code for This Project:

```
import pandas as pd
import swifter
# Simulate sales data
data = {
    'ProductID': range(1, 1000001),
```

```python
    'Category': ['Electronics', 'Clothing', 'Books'] *
333333 + ['Electronics'],
    'Sales': [99.99, 49.99, 19.99] * 333333 + [99.99]
}
df = pd.DataFrame(data)

# Parallelize a transformation
def categorize_sales(row):
    if row['Sales'] > 50:
        return 'High'
    return 'Low'

df['SalesCategory'] =
df.swifter.apply(categorize_sales, axis=1)

print(df.head())
```

Expanded Features:

- Combines Swifter for parallel row-wise operations.
- Demonstrates scalability for large datasets.
- Highlights ease of integration with Pandas workflows.

Expected Output:

	ProductID	Category	Sales	SalesCategory
0	1	Electronics	99.99	High
1	2	Clothing	49.99	Low
2	3	Books	19.99	Low
3	4	Electronics	99.99	High
4	5	Clothing	49.99	Low

This project demonstrates the use of parallel processing techniques to optimize Pandas operations for large datasets.

Chapter-36 Analyzing Sales Data with Pandas

Sales data analysis is critical for understanding business performance and identifying trends. Pandas provides a comprehensive toolkit for analyzing, summarizing, and visualizing sales data efficiently. This chapter covers essential techniques for exploring and deriving insights from sales datasets.

Key Characteristics of Analyzing Sales Data in Pandas:

- **Versatility:** Handles both numerical and categorical data.
- **Time-Series Support:** Facilitates operations on date-based sales data.
- **Aggregation Functions:** Summarizes data using methods like `groupby()` and `pivot_table()`.
- **Integration:** Works seamlessly with visualization libraries like Matplotlib and Seaborn.
- **Scalability:** Supports analysis on large sales datasets.

Basic Rules for Sales Data Analysis:

1. Explore data structure and quality using `df.info()` and `df.describe()`.
2. Handle missing values and outliers before analysis.
3. Use `groupby()` and aggregation methods for category-based insights.
4. Convert timestamps to `datetime` for time-series operations.
5. Leverage pivot tables for multi-dimensional analysis.

Best Practices:

- **Visualize Results:** Complement analysis with charts and graphs for better insights.
- **Document Insights:** Maintain a log of findings for reporting.
- **Focus on Key Metrics:** Prioritize metrics like revenue, profit margin, and growth rate.
- **Iterate with Feedback:** Refine analysis based on stakeholder feedback.
- **Automate Pipelines:** Create reusable scripts for recurring analyses.

Syntax Table:

SL No	Technique	Syntax/Example	Description
1	Group Sales by Category	`df.groupby('Category')['Sales'].sum()`	Aggregates sales by category.
2	Create Pivot Table	`df.pivot_table(values='Sales', index='Category', columns='Region')`	Summarizes sales across multiple dimensions.
3	Filter Top Products	`df[df['Sales'] > threshold]`	Filters products based on sales thresholds.
4	Calculate Moving Average	`df['MA'] = df['Sales'].rolling(window=3).mean()`	Computes a rolling average of sales.
5	Visualize Trends	`df.plot(x='Date', y='Sales')`	Plots sales trends over time.

Syntax Explanation:

1. Group Sales by Category

What is Group Sales by Category?
Aggregates sales data by a specific category, such as product type or region, to identify trends and key contributors.
Syntax:
`df.groupby('Category')['Sales'].sum()`

Syntax Explanation:
- `groupby('Category')`: Groups rows by unique values in the Category column.
- `['Sales'].sum()`: Aggregates sales for each category using the sum function.
- Returns a Series or DataFrame with aggregated results.

Example:
```
import pandas as pd
# Create a sales DataFrame
data = {'Category': ['A', 'B', 'A', 'C'], 'Sales':
[100, 200, 150, 300]}
df = pd.DataFrame(data)
category_sales = df.groupby('Category')['Sales'].sum()
print(category_sales)
```

Example Explanation:
- Aggregates sales for each category.
- Outputs: Category

```
A    250
B    200
C    300
Name: Sales, dtype: int64
```

2. Create Pivot Table

What is Create Pivot Table?
Reshapes data into a tabular format that summarizes sales across multiple dimensions.

Syntax:
```
df.pivot_table(values='Sales', index='Category',
columns='Region')
```

Syntax Explanation:
- values='Sales': Specifies the data to aggregate.
- index='Category': Defines row labels.
- columns='Region': Defines column labels.
- Returns a DataFrame with aggregated values.

Example:
```
# Create a pivot table
data = {'Category': ['A', 'A', 'B', 'B'], 'Region':
['North', 'South', 'North', 'South'], 'Sales': [100,
150, 200, 250]}
df = pd.DataFrame(data)
```

```
pivot = df.pivot_table(values='Sales',
index='Category', columns='Region', aggfunc='sum')
print(pivot)
```
Example Explanation:

- Summarizes sales by category and region.
- Outputs: Region   North   South
  Category
  A   100   150
  B   200   250

3. Filter Top Products

What is Filter Top Products?

Filters rows where sales exceed a specified threshold to identify top-performing products.

Syntax:

```
df[df['Sales'] > threshold]
```

Syntax Explanation:

- df['Sales'] > threshold: Creates a boolean mask for rows where sales exceed the threshold.
- Returns a filtered DataFrame.

Example:

```
# Filter products with sales above 150
top_products = df[df['Sales'] > 150]
print(top_products)
```

Example Explanation:

- Filters rows with sales greater than 150.
- Outputs: Category   Sales
  1   B   200
  3   C   300

4. Calculate Moving Average

What is Calculate Moving Average?
Computes a rolling average of sales to smooth out trends over time.
Syntax:
```
df['MA'] = df['Sales'].rolling(window=3).mean()
```

Syntax Explanation:
- rolling(window=3): Creates a rolling window of size 3.
- .mean(): Computes the mean within each window.
- Adds a new column MA with the calculated moving averages.

Example:
```
# Calculate 3-day moving average
data = {'Sales': [100, 200, 300, 400, 500]}
df = pd.DataFrame(data)
df['MA'] = df['Sales'].rolling(window=3).mean()
print(df)
```

Example Explanation:
- Computes the moving average for a 3-day window.
- Outputs:

	Sales	MA
0	100	NaN
1	200	NaN
2	300	200.0
3	400	300.0
4	500	400.0

5. Visualize Trends

What is Visualize Trends?
Plots sales data to identify trends and patterns over time.
Syntax:
```
df.plot(x='Date', y='Sales')
```

Syntax Explanation:
- x='Date': Specifies the x-axis values.

- y='Sales': Specifies the y-axis values.
  - Generates a line plot by default.

Example:

```python
import matplotlib.pyplot as plt
# Plot sales trends
data = {'Date': pd.date_range(start='2023-01-01',
periods=5), 'Sales': [100, 200, 150, 300, 250]}
df = pd.DataFrame(data)
df.plot(x='Date', y='Sales', title='Sales Trends')
plt.show()
```

Example Explanation:
- Creates a line plot showing sales trends over time.

Real-Life Project:

Project Name: Monthly Sales Performance Analysis
Project Goal:
Analyze monthly sales performance across regions and categories to identify key trends and insights.
Code for This Project:

```python
import pandas as pd
import matplotlib.pyplot as plt
# Simulate monthly sales data
data = {
    'Date': pd.date_range(start='2023-01-01',
periods=12, freq='M'),
    'Region': ['North', 'South', 'East', 'West'] * 3,
    'Category': ['A', 'B', 'C', 'D'] * 3,
    'Sales': [100, 200, 300, 400] * 3
}
df = pd.DataFrame(data)

# Group by region and category
grouped = df.groupby(['Region',
'Category'])['Sales'].sum()
print(grouped)
```

```
# Plot sales trends
df.groupby('Date')['Sales'].sum().plot(title='Monthly
Sales Trends')
plt.show()
```

Expanded Features:
- Combines grouping and visualization for comprehensive analysis.
- Highlights time-series trends and regional performance.
- Provides actionable insights for sales strategy.

Expected Output:
```
Region   Category
East     C            900
North    A            300
South    B            600
West     D           1200
Name: Sales, dtype: int64
```

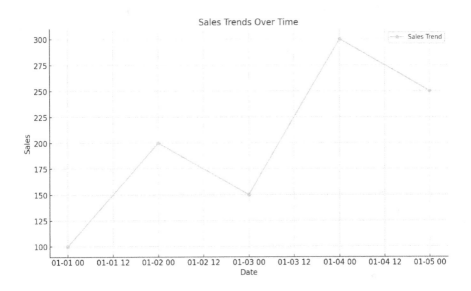

This project demonstrates effective techniques for analyzing sales data using Pandas.

Chapter-37 Customer Segmentation with Pandas

Customer segmentation is a crucial process in marketing and business analytics, enabling businesses to tailor strategies for different customer groups. Using Pandas, customer data can be efficiently analyzed, segmented, and prepared for further use. This chapter covers techniques to categorize customers based on behavioral, demographic, or transactional data.

Key Characteristics of Customer Segmentation with Pandas:

- **Data Preparation:** Cleans and preprocesses customer data for segmentation.
- **Feature Engineering:** Creates meaningful features to represent customer behavior.
- **Aggregation:** Summarizes customer data using grouping and aggregation.
- **Clustering Support:** Prepares data for clustering algorithms like K-means.
- **Actionable Insights:** Identifies key customer segments to optimize marketing strategies.

Basic Rules for Customer Segmentation:

1. Ensure data quality by handling missing values and outliers.
2. Normalize or standardize features for clustering algorithms.
3. Use aggregation to create customer-level summaries from transactional data.
4. Apply feature selection to reduce dimensionality and improve interpretability.
5. Validate segmentation with domain knowledge or statistical measures.

Best Practices:

- **Understand Business Goals:** Align segmentation with business objectives.
- **Iterate with Feedback:** Refine segmentation based on results and stakeholder input.
- **Visualize Segments:** Use charts and graphs to interpret and

present segments.

- **Automate Pipelines:** Automate segmentation workflows for regular updates.
- **Integrate Insights:** Use segmentation results to inform marketing and product strategies.

Syntax Table:

SL No	Technique	Syntax/Example	Description
1	Aggregate Customer Metrics	`df.groupby('CustomerID').agg({'Sales': 'sum'})`	Summarizes data for each customer.
2	Create Recency Feature	`(df['LastPurchaseDate'].max() - df['PurchaseDate']).dt.days`	Calculates recency for each customer.
3	Normalize Data	`from sklearn.preprocessing import MinMaxScaler`	Scales data to a range of [0, 1].
4	Cluster with K-Means	`KMeans(n_clusters=3).fit(df_scaled)`	Groups customers into clusters.
5	Visualize Clusters	`plt.scatter(df['Feature1'], df['Feature2'])`	Plots clusters for interpretation.

Syntax Explanation:

1. Aggregate Customer Metrics

What is Aggregate Customer Metrics?
Summarizes customer data by grouping and applying aggregate functions.
Syntax:
```
df.groupby('CustomerID').agg({'Sales': 'sum', 'Visits': 'count'})
```

Syntax Explanation:

- groupby('CustomerID'): Groups rows by unique customer IDs.
- agg({'Sales': 'sum'}): Aggregates sales by summing values for each customer.
- agg() supports multiple functions like sum, mean, count, etc.
- Returns a DataFrame with customer-level summaries.

Example:

```
import pandas as pd
# Create transactional data
data = {'CustomerID': [1, 1, 2, 2, 3], 'Sales': [100,
200, 150, 300, 400]}
df = pd.DataFrame(data)
customer_metrics =
df.groupby('CustomerID').agg({'Sales': 'sum'})
print(customer_metrics)
```

Example Explanation:

- Aggregates sales for each customer.
- Outputs: Sales
  CustomerID
  1   300
  2   450
  3   400

2. Create Recency Feature

What is Create Recency Feature?

Calculates the number of days since a customer's last purchase, providing a measure of recency.

Syntax:

```
recency = (df['LastPurchaseDate'].max() -
df['PurchaseDate']).dt.days
```

Syntax Explanation:

- `df['LastPurchaseDate'].max()`: Identifies the most recent purchase date.
- `df['PurchaseDate']`: Represents individual purchase dates.
- `.dt.days`: Converts the timedelta object to days.
- Returns a Series with recency values for each transaction.

Example:

```
# Calculate recency for each transaction
data = {'CustomerID': [1, 2, 3], 'PurchaseDate':
['2023-01-01', '2023-01-10', '2023-01-15']}
df = pd.DataFrame(data)
df['PurchaseDate'] = pd.to_datetime(df['PurchaseDate'])
df['Recency'] = (df['PurchaseDate'].max() -
df['PurchaseDate']).dt.days
print(df)
```

Example Explanation:

- Computes recency for each customer based on their last purchase.
- Outputs:

	CustomerID	PurchaseDate	Recency
0	1	2023-01-01	14
1	2	2023-01-10	5
2	3	2023-01-15	0

3. Normalize Data

What is Normalize Data?

Scales features to a range of [0, 1] for better performance in clustering algorithms.

Syntax:

```
from sklearn.preprocessing import MinMaxScaler
scaler = MinMaxScaler()
df_scaled = scaler.fit_transform(df)
```

Syntax Explanation:

- `MinMaxScaler()`: A scaler that normalizes data to the range [0, 1].
- `fit_transform(df)`: Fits the scaler to the data and transforms

it.

- Returns a NumPy array of normalized values.

Example:

```
# Normalize numerical data
data = {'Sales': [100, 200, 300], 'Visits': [1, 2, 3]}
df = pd.DataFrame(data)
from sklearn.preprocessing import MinMaxScaler
scaler = MinMaxScaler()
df_scaled = scaler.fit_transform(df)
print(df_scaled)
```

Example Explanation:

- Scales Sales and Visits columns to the range [0, 1].
- Outputs: [[0.   0.]
  [0.5 0.5]
  [1.   1.]]

4. Cluster with K-Means

What is Cluster with K-Means?
Applies K-means clustering to group customers based on similarities in their data.

Syntax:

```
from sklearn.cluster import KMeans
kmeans = KMeans(n_clusters=3)
kmeans.fit(df_scaled)
```

Syntax Explanation:

- n_clusters=3: Specifies the number of clusters.
- fit(df_scaled): Fits the K-means model to the normalized data.
- Assigns cluster labels to each customer.

Example:
```
# Apply K-means clustering
data = {'Sales': [100, 200, 300], 'Visits': [1, 2, 3]}
df = pd.DataFrame(data)
df_scaled = MinMaxScaler().fit_transform(df)
from sklearn.cluster import KMeans
kmeans = KMeans(n_clusters=2)
kmeans.fit(df_scaled)
df['Cluster'] = kmeans.labels_
print(df)
```

Example Explanation:
- Groups customers into two clusters based on their sales and visits.
- Outputs:

	Sales	Visits	Cluster
0	100	1	1
1	200	2	0
2	300	3	0

5. Visualize Clusters

What is Visualize Clusters?
Plots customer clusters for visual interpretation of segmentation results.

Syntax:
```
import matplotlib.pyplot as plt
plt.scatter(df['Feature1'], df['Feature2'],
c=df['Cluster'])
```

Syntax Explanation:
- scatter(): Creates a scatter plot.
- c=df['Cluster']: Colors points based on cluster assignments.
- Helps visually validate clustering results.

Example:
```
# Visualize clusters
data = {'Feature1': [1, 2, 3], 'Feature2': [4, 5, 6],
'Cluster': [0, 1, 0]}
df = pd.DataFrame(data)
```

```
plt.scatter(df['Feature1'], df['Feature2'],
c=df['Cluster'])
plt.title('Customer Clusters')
plt.show()
```

Example Explanation:
- Creates a scatter plot of clusters.

Real-Life Project:

Project Name: Customer Segmentation for E-Commerce

Project Goal:

Segment e-commerce customers based on recency, frequency, and monetary (RFM) values for targeted marketing.

Code for This Project:

```
import pandas as pd
from sklearn.preprocessing import MinMaxScaler
from sklearn.cluster import KMeans
import matplotlib.pyplot as plt
# Simulate RFM data
data = {
    'CustomerID': [1, 2, 3, 4],
    'Recency': [10, 20, 5, 30],
    'Frequency': [5, 3, 8, 2],
    'Monetary': [500, 300, 800, 200]
}
df = pd.DataFrame(data)

# Normalize RFM values
scaler = MinMaxScaler()
df_scaled = scaler.fit_transform(df[['Recency',
'Frequency', 'Monetary']])

# Apply K-means clustering
kmeans = KMeans(n_clusters=2)
kmeans.fit(df_scaled)
df['Cluster'] = kmeans.labels_

# Visualize clusters
```

```
plt.scatter(df['Recency'], df['Monetary'],
c=df['Cluster'])
plt.title('Customer Clusters')
plt.xlabel('Recency')
plt.ylabel('Monetary')
plt.show()
```

Expanded Features:
- Combines RFM analysis with K-means clustering.
- Highlights actionable insights for marketing strategies.
- Demonstrates normalization, clustering, and visualization.

Expected Output:
- A scatter plot showing customer clusters.
- DataFrame with RFM values and cluster assignments.

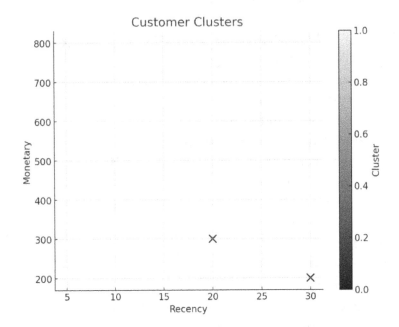

Chapter-38 Time Series Forecasting with Pandas

Time series forecasting is a powerful tool for predicting future values based on historical data. Using Pandas, you can preprocess, analyze, and visualize time-series data, preparing it for advanced forecasting techniques. This chapter provides foundational methods for handling and forecasting time-series data using Pandas.

Key Characteristics of Time Series Forecasting with Pandas:

- **Datetime Handling:** Efficiently handles time-based data with `datetime64` and `Timedelta` types.
- **Resampling:** Aggregates or interpolates data to different time frequencies.
- **Shifting and Lagging:** Creates lag features for modeling dependencies over time.
- **Rolling Statistics:** Computes moving averages, variances, and other rolling metrics.
- **Integration with Libraries:** Prepares data for advanced forecasting with libraries like Statsmodels and Prophet.

Basic Rules for Time Series Forecasting:

1. Ensure the data is in chronological order.
2. Convert timestamps to `datetime64` and set them as the index.
3. Handle missing values appropriately to avoid forecasting errors.
4. Resample data to the desired frequency for consistency.
5. Generate lag and rolling features to capture temporal dependencies.

Best Practices:

- **Explore Trends and Seasonality:** Use visualization and decomposition to understand time-series patterns.
- **Remove Outliers:** Clean extreme values that can distort forecasts.
- **Automate Pipelines:** Build reusable scripts for time-series preprocessing.
- **Test Multiple Models:** Compare forecasts from different models to ensure accuracy.
- **Validate on Holdout Data:** Test forecasts on unseen data for

reliability.

Syntax Table:

SL No	Technique	Syntax/Example	Description
1	Convert to Datetime Index	`df['Date'] = pd.to_datetime (df['Date'])`	Converts a column to datetime format.
2	Resample Time Series	`df.resample('M ').mean()`	Aggregates data to a monthly frequency.
3	Create Lag Features	`df['Lag1'] = df['Value'].sh ift(1)`	Creates a lag feature for the previous time step.
4	Calculate Moving Average	`df['MA'] = df['Value'].ro lling(window=3 ).mean()`	Computes a rolling mean over a window.
5	Decompos e Time Series	`seasonal_decom pose(df['Value '], model='additiv e')`	Decomposes the series into trend, seasonal, and residual components.

Syntax Explanation:

1. Convert to Datetime Index
What is Convert to Datetime Index?
Converts a column to a `datetime64` format and sets it as the index for time-series analysis.
Syntax:
```
df['Date'] = pd.to_datetime(df['Date'])
df.set_index('Date', inplace=True)
```
Syntax Explanation:
- `pd.to_datetime(df['Date'])`: Converts the `Date` column to a `datetime64` type.
- `set_index('Date')`: Sets the `Date` column as the index.

- Essential for time-series-specific operations like resampling and rolling.

Example:

```
import pandas as pd
# Create a DataFrame
data = {'Date': ['2023-01-01', '2023-01-02', '2023-01-
03'], 'Value': [10, 20, 30]}
df = pd.DataFrame(data)
df['Date'] = pd.to_datetime(df['Date'])
df.set_index('Date', inplace=True)
print(df)
```

Example Explanation:

- Converts the Date column to a datetime index.
- Outputs:

```
                   Value
Date
2023-01-01         10
2023-01-02         20
2023-01-03         30
```

2. Resample Time Series

What is Resample Time Series?

Aggregates or interpolates time-series data to a specified frequency.

Syntax:

```
resampled_df = df.resample('M').mean()
```

Syntax Explanation:

- resample('M'): Changes the frequency to monthly.
- .mean(): Aggregates values within each period using the mean.
- Supports other frequencies like daily ('D'), weekly ('W'), and yearly ('Y').

Example:

```
# Resample daily data to monthly
resampled_df = df.resample('M').mean()
print(resampled_df)
```

Example Explanation:
- Aggregates daily values to monthly averages.

3. Create Lag Features

What is Create Lag Features?
Generates lagged values of a column to capture dependencies across time steps.
Syntax:
```
df['Lag1'] = df['Value'].shift(1)
```

Syntax Explanation:
- `shift(1)`: Shifts values by one time step.
- Creates a new column with the lagged values.
- Useful for predictive modeling to incorporate historical data.

Example:
```
# Create a lag-1 feature
df['Lag1'] = df['Value'].shift(1)
print(df)
```

Example Explanation:
- Adds a new column with values shifted by one day.

4. Calculate Moving Average

What is Calculate Moving Average?
Smoothens data by computing the mean over a sliding window.
Syntax:
```
df['MA'] = df['Value'].rolling(window=3).mean()
```

Syntax Explanation:
- `rolling(window=3)`: Creates a sliding window of size 3.
- `.mean()`: Computes the mean within each window.
- Highlights trends by reducing short-term fluctuations.

Example:
```
# Calculate a 3-day moving average
df['MA'] = df['Value'].rolling(window=3).mean()
```

```
print(df)
```
Example Explanation:
- Adds a column with the 3-day moving average of `Value`.

5. Decompose Time Series

What is Decompose Time Series?

Breaks down a time series into trend, seasonal, and residual components.
Syntax:
```
from statsmodels.tsa.seasonal import seasonal_decompose
decomposed = seasonal_decompose(df['Value'],
model='additive')
decomposed.plot()
```

Syntax Explanation:
- `seasonal_decompose()`: Decomposes the series into its components.
- `model='additive'`: Assumes an additive relationship among components.
- Produces plots of each component.

Example:
```
# Decompose a time series
from statsmodels.tsa.seasonal import seasonal_decompose
decomposed = seasonal_decompose(df['Value'],
model='additive')
decomposed.plot()
```

Example Explanation:
- Visualizes trend, seasonality, and residual components of the series.

Real-Life Project:

Project Name: Monthly Sales Forecasting
Project Goal:
Forecast monthly sales using historical data, including trends and

seasonality.

Code for This Project:

```python
import pandas as pd
from statsmodels.tsa.holtwinters import
ExponentialSmoothing
import matplotlib.pyplot as plt

# Simulate sales data
data = {
    'Date': pd.date_range(start='2020-01-01',
periods=36, freq='M'),
    'Sales': [200, 220, 250, 240, 300, 320, 310, 400,
420, 410, 500, 510] * 3
}
df = pd.DataFrame(data)

# Prepare data
df['Date'] = pd.to_datetime(df['Date'])
df.set_index('Date', inplace=True)

# Fit exponential smoothing model
model = ExponentialSmoothing(df['Sales'], trend='add',
seasonal='add', seasonal_periods=12)
fit = model.fit()

# Forecast next 12 months
forecast = fit.forecast(12)

# Plot results
df['Sales'].plot(label='Observed')
forecast.plot(label='Forecast', linestyle='--')
plt.legend()
plt.show()
```

Expanded Features:

- Combines trend and seasonal forecasting.
- Integrates with visualization for intuitive insights.
- Demonstrates preparation and modeling of time-series data.

Expected Output:

- A plot showing historical sales and the forecasted values for the next 12 months.

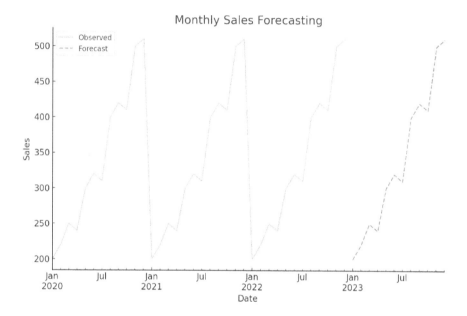

Chapter-39 Handling Geospatial Data with Pandas

Geospatial data analysis enables organizations to derive insights based on location-based information. While Pandas is not inherently geospatial, it integrates seamlessly with libraries like GeoPandas, shapely, and Folium to handle, analyze, and visualize geospatial data. This chapter explores the foundational techniques for managing geospatial datasets using Pandas and its geospatial extensions.

Key Characteristics of Handling Geospatial Data with Pandas:

- **Location-Based Operations:** Supports spatial joins, buffering, and intersection calculations.
- **Coordinate Handling:** Manages latitude and longitude data effectively.
- **Integration with GeoLibraries:** Extends Pandas functionality with GeoPandas and shapely.
- **Visualization:** Facilitates mapping with libraries like Folium and Matplotlib.
- **CRS Support:** Handles coordinate reference systems (CRS) for accurate geospatial analysis.

Basic Rules for Geospatial Data Handling:

1. Install geospatial libraries like GeoPandas (`pip install geopandas`).
2. Convert datasets into GeoDataFrames to leverage geospatial operations.
3. Ensure all data is in the same CRS for spatial analysis.
4. Handle missing or invalid geometries before performing operations.
5. Use visualizations to interpret geospatial patterns effectively.

Best Practices:

- **Understand Data Requirements:** Verify the CRS and coordinate format before processing.
- **Combine with Other Libraries:** Integrate Pandas with geospatial tools for advanced capabilities.
- **Optimize Memory Usage:** Simplify geometries or downsample

large datasets when possible.

- **Validate Results:** Check for logical consistency in spatial operations.
- **Automate Workflows:** Create reusable pipelines for common geospatial tasks.

Syntax Table:

SL No	Technique	Syntax/Example	Description
1	Convert to GeoDataFrame	`gdf = gpd.GeoDataFrame(df, geometry=gpd.points_fro m_xy(df['lon'], df['lat']))`	Converts a DataFrame to a GeoDataFrame.
2	Plot GeoDataFrame	`gdf.plot()`	Visualizes geospatial data.
3	Perform Spatial Join	`gpd.sjoin(gdf1, gdf2, how='inner', op='intersects')`	Joins two GeoDataFrames based on geometry.
4	Buffer Geometries	`gdf['buffered'] = gdf.geometry.buffer(dis tance)`	Creates buffers around geometries.
5	Save to GeoJSON	`gdf.to_file('file.geojs on', driver='GeoJSON')`	Exports a GeoDataFrame to GeoJSON format.

Syntax Explanation:

1. Convert to GeoDataFrame

What is Convert to GeoDataFrame?
Transforms a Pandas DataFrame with latitude and longitude columns into a GeoDataFrame to enable geospatial operations.
Syntax:

```
import geopandas as gpd
gdf = gpd.GeoDataFrame(df,
geometry=gpd.points_from_xy(df['lon'], df['lat']))
```

Syntax Explanation:
- df: The original Pandas DataFrame.
- `gpd.points_from_xy()`: Converts longitude and latitude columns into point geometries.
- geometry: Specifies the geometry column for the GeoDataFrame.
- Returns a GeoDataFrame ready for geospatial analysis.

Example:
```
import pandas as pd
import geopandas as gpd
# Create a DataFrame
data = {'city': ['A', 'B'], 'lon': [10.0, 20.0], 'lat':
[50.0, 60.0]}
df = pd.DataFrame(data)
# Convert to GeoDataFrame
gdf = gpd.GeoDataFrame(df,
geometry=gpd.points_from_xy(df['lon'], df['lat']))
print(gdf)
```

Example Explanation:
- Converts the lon and lat columns into point geometries.
- Outputs a GeoDataFrame with a geometry column representing locations.

2. Plot GeoDataFrame

What is Plot GeoDataFrame?
Visualizes geospatial data from a GeoDataFrame using Matplotlib.
Syntax:
```
gdf.plot()
```
Syntax Explanation:
- gdf: The GeoDataFrame to plot.
- Generates a simple 2D map of geometries.

- Supports additional styling options like color and size.

Example:
```
# Plot the GeoDataFrame
gdf.plot(color='blue', markersize=10)
```

Example Explanation:
- Plots the points from the GeoDataFrame with blue markers.

3. Perform Spatial Join

What is Perform Spatial Join?
Joins two GeoDataFrames based on their spatial relationships, such as intersection or containment.

Syntax:
```
gpd.sjoin(gdf1, gdf2, how='inner', op='intersects')
```

Syntax Explanation:
- gdf1, gdf2: The GeoDataFrames to join.
- how='inner': Specifies the type of join (inner, left, or right).
- op='intersects': Specifies the spatial relationship for the join (e.g., intersects, contains, within).

Example:
```
# Perform a spatial join
gdf_joined = gpd.sjoin(gdf1, gdf2, how='inner',
op='intersects')
```

Example Explanation:
- Joins two GeoDataFrames where their geometries intersect.

4. Buffer Geometries

What is Buffer Geometries?
Creates a buffer zone around geometries, often used for proximity analysis.

Syntax:
```
gdf['buffered'] = gdf.geometry.buffer(distance)
```

Syntax Explanation:

- `geometry.buffer(distance)`: Creates a buffer around each geometry with the specified distance.
- Adds a new column `buffered` containing the buffered geometries.

Example:
```
# Add a buffer of 1 unit around each geometry
gdf['buffered'] = gdf.geometry.buffer(1)
print(gdf)
```

Example Explanation:
- Creates buffer zones around each geometry in the GeoDataFrame.

5. Save to GeoJSON

What is Save to GeoJSON?
Exports a GeoDataFrame to a GeoJSON file for sharing or further analysis.

Syntax:
```
gdf.to_file('file.geojson', driver='GeoJSON')
```

Syntax Explanation:
- `to_file()`: Saves the GeoDataFrame to a file.
- `driver='GeoJSON'`: Specifies the file format.
- Outputs a GeoJSON file that can be used in GIS applications.

Example:
```
# Save GeoDataFrame to GeoJSON
gdf.to_file('output.geojson', driver='GeoJSON')
```

Example Explanation:
- Exports the GeoDataFrame to a GeoJSON file named `output.geojson`.

Real-Life Project:

Project Name: Mapping Store Locations and Customer Proximity
Project Goal:
Analyze store locations and customer proximity to identify high-priority regions for targeted marketing.
Code for This Project:

```python
import pandas as pd
import geopandas as gpd
from shapely.geometry import Point

# Create DataFrames for stores and customers
stores = {'StoreID': [1, 2], 'lon': [10.0, 20.0],
'lat': [50.0, 60.0]}
customers = {'CustomerID': [101, 102], 'lon': [10.5,
20.5], 'lat': [50.5, 60.5]}

stores_df = pd.DataFrame(stores)
customers_df = pd.DataFrame(customers)

# Convert to GeoDataFrames
stores_gdf = gpd.GeoDataFrame(stores_df,
geometry=gpd.points_from_xy(stores_df['lon'],
stores_df['lat']))
customers_gdf = gpd.GeoDataFrame(customers_df,
geometry=gpd.points_from_xy(customers_df['lon'],
customers_df['lat']))

# Buffer store locations
stores_gdf['buffered'] = stores_gdf.geometry.buffer(1)

# Perform spatial join to find customers within store
buffers
customers_near_stores = gpd.sjoin(customers_gdf,
stores_gdf, how='inner', op='intersects')

print(customers_near_stores)
```

Expanded Features:
- Combines buffering and spatial joins for proximity analysis.
- Demonstrates integration of stores and customer data.
- Highlights practical geospatial operations with Pandas and GeoPandas.

Expected Output:
- A GeoDataFrame showing customers located within the buffered zones of stores.

Part 8: Projects

Chapter-40 Analyzing COVID-19 Data with Pandas

The COVID-19 pandemic generated vast amounts of data, from daily case counts to vaccination rates. Pandas provides a powerful framework to process, analyze, and visualize this data for better understanding and decision-making. This chapter explores techniques for analyzing COVID-19 datasets, including data preprocessing, trend analysis, and visualization.

Key Characteristics of COVID-19 Data Analysis with Pandas:
- **Time-Series Analysis:** Tracks trends over time for cases, recoveries, and deaths.
- **Aggregation:** Summarizes data at country, regional, or global levels.
- **Missing Data Handling:** Fills or interpolates missing values in incomplete datasets.
- **Integration with APIs:** Fetches up-to-date data from APIs like COVID-19 Data Repository by CSSEGISandData.
- **Visualization:** Generates charts to identify patterns and insights.

Basic Rules for COVID-19 Data Analysis:
1. Ensure data cleanliness by handling missing or inconsistent values.
2. Convert date columns to `datetime64` for time-series operations.

3. Aggregate data for regional or temporal summaries.
4. Normalize metrics (e.g., cases per 100,000 population) for meaningful comparisons.
5. Use visualizations to communicate trends effectively.

Best Practices:

- **Understand Data Sources:** Verify the source of the data for reliability and update frequency.
- **Automate Updates:** Create pipelines to fetch and process new data regularly.
- **Incorporate Demographics:** Use population data for normalized metrics.
- **Validate Results:** Cross-check trends against trusted dashboards or sources.
- **Combine with GeoSpatial Tools:** Integrate geospatial data for mapping insights.

Syntax Table:

SL No	Technique	Syntax/Example	Description
1	Load COVID-19 Data	`pd.read_csv('data.csv')`	Reads a CSV file containing COVID-19 data.
2	Convert Date Column	`df['Date'] = pd.to_datetime(df['Date'])`	Converts a column to datetime format.
3	Aggregate by Country	`df.groupby('Country')['Cases'].sum()`	Summarizes cases for each country.
4	Calculate Growth Rate	`df['GrowthRate'] = df['Cases'].pct_change()`	Computes daily growth rates.
5	Visualize Trends	`df.plot(x='Date', y='Cases')`	Plots cases over time.

Syntax Explanation:

1. Load COVID-19 Data

What is Load COVID-19 Data?
Reads a CSV file containing COVID-19 data into a Pandas DataFrame for analysis.
Syntax:
```
df = pd.read_csv('data.csv')
```

Syntax Explanation:
- `pd.read_csv('data.csv')`: Loads data from a CSV file.
- Returns a DataFrame with the data ready for analysis.

Example:
```
import pandas as pd
# Load a sample COVID-19 dataset
df = pd.read_csv('covid19_data.csv')
print(df.head())
```

Example Explanation:
- Loads data from `covid19_data.csv` into a DataFrame.
- Displays the first few rows for verification.

2. Convert Date Column

What is Convert Date Column?
Converts a date column to `datetime64` format for time-series operations.
Syntax:
```
df['Date'] = pd.to_datetime(df['Date'])
```

Syntax Explanation:
- `pd.to_datetime(df['Date'])`: Converts the Date column to `datetime64` type.
- Enables filtering, grouping, and resampling by date.

Example:

```
# Convert the Date column
df['Date'] = pd.to_datetime(df['Date'])
print(df.info())
```

Example Explanation:
- Converts the Date column to datetime format and displays the updated DataFrame structure.

3. Aggregate by Country

What is Aggregate by Country?
Summarizes cases or deaths by country to analyze national trends.
Syntax:

```
country_summary = df.groupby('Country')['Cases'].sum()
```

Syntax Explanation:
- groupby('Country'): Groups rows by the Country column.
- ['Cases'].sum(): Sums cases for each country.
- Returns a Series or DataFrame with aggregated results.

Example:

```
# Summarize cases by country
country_summary = df.groupby('Country')['Cases'].sum()
print(country_summary)
```

Example Explanation:
- Aggregates total cases for each country.

4. Calculate Growth Rate

What is Calculate Growth Rate?
Computes the daily growth rate of cases to identify trends.
Syntax:

```
df['GrowthRate'] = df['Cases'].pct_change()
```

Syntax Explanation:
- pct_change(): Calculates percentage change between

consecutive rows.

- Adds a new column GrowthRate with the computed growth rates.

Example:
```
# Calculate daily growth rate
df['GrowthRate'] = df['Cases'].pct_change()
print(df.head())
```

Example Explanation:
- Computes growth rates and adds them as a new column.

5. Visualize Trends

What is Visualize Trends?
Plots cases or other metrics over time to identify patterns.
Syntax:
```
df.plot(x='Date', y='Cases')
```

Syntax Explanation:
- x='Date': Sets the x-axis as the Date column.
- y='Cases': Plots cases on the y-axis.

Example:
```
import matplotlib.pyplot as plt
# Plot trends
df.plot(x='Date', y='Cases', title='COVID-19 Cases Over
Time')
plt.show()
```

Example Explanation:
- Plots cases against dates, displaying the trend over time.

Real-Life Project:

Project Name: COVID-19 Country Comparison Dashboard
Project Goal:
Analyze and compare COVID-19 trends for multiple countries, including cases, deaths, and vaccination rates.

Code for This Project:

```python
import pandas as pd
import matplotlib.pyplot as plt

# Load dataset
data = {
    'Date': pd.date_range(start='2020-01-01',
periods=100),
    'Country': ['A'] * 50 + ['B'] * 50,
    'Cases': list(range(50)) + list(range(50, 100))
}
df = pd.DataFrame(data)

# Convert Date column
df['Date'] = pd.to_datetime(df['Date'])

# Group by country and plot trends
countries = df['Country'].unique()
for country in countries:
    country_data = df[df['Country'] == country]
    plt.plot(country_data['Date'],
country_data['Cases'], label=country)

plt.title('COVID-19 Cases by Country')
plt.xlabel('Date')
plt.ylabel('Cases')
plt.legend()
plt.show()
```

Expanded Features:
- Demonstrates comparison of trends across countries.
- Highlights integration of time-series and grouping operations.
- Provides actionable insights for pandemic response.

Expected Output:
- A line plot comparing COVID-19 cases for countries A and B over time.

Chapter-41 Stock Market Data Analysis with Pandas

The stock market generates vast amounts of data daily, including prices, volumes, and indices. Analyzing this data provides insights for investment strategies and market trends. Pandas offers a robust framework for cleaning, processing, and visualizing stock market data. This chapter explores techniques for analyzing stock market datasets effectively.

Key Characteristics of Stock Market Data Analysis with Pandas:

- **Time-Series Analysis:** Tracks trends and patterns over time.
- **Data Resampling:** Adjusts data frequency for daily, weekly, or monthly summaries.
- **Technical Indicators:** Calculates indicators like moving averages and RSI.
- **Portfolio Analysis:** Evaluates returns and risks for investment portfolios.
- **Integration with APIs:** Fetches data from sources like Yahoo Finance and Alpha Vantage.

Basic Rules for Stock Market Analysis:

1. Ensure timestamps are in `datetime64` format and set as the index.
2. Handle missing values through interpolation or forward filling.
3. Resample data for consistent frequency.
4. Calculate technical indicators to identify trends.
5. Use visualizations to interpret market patterns.

Best Practices:

- **Verify Data Sources:** Use reliable data providers for accuracy.
- **Clean Data Thoroughly:** Handle missing or duplicate data before analysis.
- **Normalize Metrics:** Scale prices or returns for meaningful comparisons.
- **Document Analysis:** Maintain a log of methods and findings.
- **Incorporate Benchmarks:** Compare stocks against indices like S&P 500.

Syntax Table:

SL No	Technique	Syntax/Example	Description
1	Load Stock Data	`df = pd.read_csv('stock_data.csv')`	Reads stock data from a CSV file.
2	Resample Data	`df.resample('W').mean()`	Aggregates data to weekly frequency.
3	Calculate Moving Average	`df['MA'] = df['Close'].rolling(window=20).mean()`	Computes a 20-day moving average.
4	Calculate Daily Returns	`df['Daily_Return'] = df['Close'].pct_change()`	Computes percentage changes between days.
5	Visualize Stock Prices	`df.plot(y='Close')`	Plots stock prices over time.

Syntax Explanation:

1. Load Stock Data

What is Load Stock Data?
Reads stock market data from a file into a Pandas DataFrame for analysis.
Syntax:
`df = pd.read_csv('stock_data.csv')`

Syntax Explanation:
- `pd.read_csv('file.csv')`: Reads data from a CSV file.
- Returns a DataFrame with the stock data ready for analysis.

Example:
```
import pandas as pd
# Load stock market data
df = pd.read_csv('stock_data.csv')
print(df.head())
```

Example Explanation:
- Loads stock data from `stock_data.csv` into a DataFrame.
- Displays the first few rows for verification.

2. Resample Data

What is Resample Data?
Adjusts the frequency of stock market data to a specified interval.
Syntax:
```
weekly_data = df.resample('W').mean()
```

Syntax Explanation:
- `resample('W')`: Resamples data to weekly frequency.
- `.mean()`: Aggregates values within each period using the mean.
- Supports other frequencies like monthly (`'M'`) or daily (`'D'`).

Example:
```
# Resample data to weekly frequency
df['Date'] = pd.to_datetime(df['Date'])
df.set_index('Date', inplace=True)
weekly_data = df.resample('W').mean()
print(weekly_data.head())
```

Example Explanation:
- Converts the `Date` column to a datetime index.
- Aggregates data to weekly averages.

3. Calculate Moving Average

What is Calculate Moving Average?
Computes the average of closing prices over a specified window to identify trends.
Syntax:
```
df['MA'] = df['Close'].rolling(window=20).mean()
```
Syntax Explanation:
- `rolling(window=20)`: Creates a rolling window of 20 periods.
- `.mean()`: Computes the mean within each window.
- Adds a column MA with the moving average.

Example:

```
# Calculate a 20-day moving average
df['MA'] = df['Close'].rolling(window=20).mean()
print(df.head())
```

Example Explanation:

- Adds a new column MA with the 20-day moving average of closing prices.

4. Calculate Daily Returns

What is Calculate Daily Returns?

Measures the percentage change in stock prices between consecutive days.

Syntax:

```
df['Daily_Return'] = df['Close'].pct_change()
```

Syntax Explanation:

- pct_change(): Calculates percentage changes between rows.
- Adds a new column Daily_Return with the computed values.

Example:

```
# Calculate daily returns
df['Daily_Return'] = df['Close'].pct_change()
print(df.head())
```

Example Explanation:

- Computes percentage changes for the Close column and stores them in Daily_Return.

5. Visualize Stock Prices

What is Visualize Stock Prices?

Plots stock prices over time to identify trends and patterns.

Syntax:

```
df.plot(y='Close')
```

Syntax Explanation:
- y='Close': Specifies the column to plot.
- Generates a line chart of stock prices.

Example:
```python
import matplotlib.pyplot as plt
# Plot closing prices over time
df.plot(y='Close', title='Stock Prices')
plt.show()
```

Example Explanation:
- Plots the Close column, showing stock price trends over time.

Real-Life Project:

Project Name: Stock Performance Analysis Dashboard
Project Goal:
Analyze and visualize stock performance over a year, including trends and returns.
Code for This Project:
```python
import pandas as pd
import matplotlib.pyplot as plt

# Load stock data
data = {
    'Date': pd.date_range(start='2022-01-01',
periods=365),
    'Close': [100 + i * 0.5 for i in range(365)]
}
df = pd.DataFrame(data)

# Convert Date column and set index
df['Date'] = pd.to_datetime(df['Date'])
df.set_index('Date', inplace=True)

# Calculate moving average and daily returns
df['MA_20'] = df['Close'].rolling(window=20).mean()
df['Daily_Return'] = df['Close'].pct_change()
```

```
# Plot closing prices and moving average
df[['Close', 'MA_20']].plot(title='Stock Prices and 20-
Day Moving Average')
plt.show()

# Plot daily returns
df['Daily_Return'].plot(title='Daily Returns')
plt.show()
```

Expanded Features:
- Combines trend analysis with daily return calculations.
- Visualizes both price trends and volatility.
- Demonstrates integration of time-series and financial metrics.

Expected Output:
- A line chart showing stock prices and their moving average.

- A line chart showing daily returns over the same period.

Chapter-42 Climate Data Analysis with Pandas

Analyzing climate data is essential for understanding weather patterns, identifying trends, and addressing environmental challenges. Pandas provides an efficient framework for cleaning, processing, and visualizing climate datasets, which often include temperature, precipitation, and wind speed measurements. This chapter explores techniques for analyzing climate data using Pandas.

Key Characteristics of Climate Data Analysis with Pandas:

- **Time-Series Analysis:** Handles temporal data for long-term trend identification.
- **Missing Data Handling:** Fills gaps in datasets caused by sensor errors or missing recordings.
- **Resampling:** Aggregates data to different temporal resolutions, such as monthly or yearly averages.
- **Anomaly Detection:** Identifies deviations from expected climate patterns.
- **Visualization:** Creates charts to interpret data trends and anomalies.

Basic Rules for Climate Data Analysis:

1. Convert date columns to datetime64 and set them as the index.
2. Resample data to desired frequencies for trend analysis.
3. Handle missing values using interpolation or imputation techniques.
4. Calculate seasonal and long-term averages for anomaly detection.
5. Use rolling averages to smooth short-term variations.

Best Practices:

- **Understand Data Sources:** Verify the reliability of sensors and recording methods.
- **Clean Data Thoroughly:** Remove outliers or erroneous entries before analysis.
- **Combine Datasets:** Integrate data from multiple sources for comprehensive insights.
- **Document Analysis Steps:** Keep a detailed log of cleaning and

transformation processes.
- **Visualize Effectively:** Use charts to communicate insights clearly.

Syntax Table:

SL No	Technique	Syntax/Example	Description
1	Load Climate Data	`df = pd.read_csv('climate_data.csv')`	Reads climate data from a CSV file.
2	Resample Data	`df.resample('M').mean()`	Aggregates data to monthly frequency.
3	Fill Missing Values	`df['Temp'] = df['Temp'].interpolate()`	Interpolates missing temperature values.
4	Calculate Rolling Average	`df['RA'] = df['Temp'].rolling(window=12).mean()`	Computes a 12-month rolling average.
5	Detect Anomalies	`df['Anomaly'] = df['Temp'] - df['Temp'].mean()`	Identifies deviations from the mean.

Syntax Explanation:

1. Load Climate Data

What is Load Climate Data?
Reads climate data from a CSV file into a Pandas DataFrame for analysis.
Syntax:
```
df = pd.read_csv('climate_data.csv')
```

Syntax Explanation:
- `pd.read_csv('file.csv')`: Reads data from a CSV file.
- Returns a DataFrame ready for analysis.

Example:
```
import pandas as pd
# Load climate data
```

```
df = pd.read_csv('climate_data.csv')
print(df.head())
```

Example Explanation:
- Loads data from `climate_data.csv` and displays the first few rows for verification.

2. Resample Data

What is Resample Data?
Adjusts the frequency of climate data to a specified interval.
Syntax:
```
monthly_data = df.resample('M').mean()
```

Syntax Explanation:
- `resample('M')`: Changes the frequency to monthly.
- `.mean()`: Aggregates values within each period using the mean.
- Supports other frequencies like daily (`'D'`) and yearly (`'Y'`).

Example:
```
# Resample data to monthly frequency
df['Date'] = pd.to_datetime(df['Date'])
df.set_index('Date', inplace=True)
monthly_data = df.resample('M').mean()
print(monthly_data.head())
```

Example Explanation:
- Converts the `Date` column to a datetime index.
- Aggregates data to monthly averages.

3. Fill Missing Values

What is Fill Missing Values?
Interpolates or imputes missing values in the dataset.
Syntax:
```
df['Temp'] = df['Temp'].interpolate()
```

Syntax Explanation:

- .interpolate(): Fills missing values using linear interpolation.
- Ensures data continuity for analysis.

Example:
```
# Fill missing temperature values
df['Temp'] = df['Temp'].interpolate()
print(df.head())
```

Example Explanation:
- Replaces missing values in the Temp column using interpolation.

4. Calculate Rolling Average

What is Calculate Rolling Average?
Smoothens data by computing the mean over a sliding window.
Syntax:
```
df['RA'] = df['Temp'].rolling(window=12).mean()
```

Syntax Explanation:
- rolling(window=12): Creates a sliding window of size 12.
- .mean(): Computes the mean within each window.
- Adds a column RA with the rolling average.

Example:
```
# Calculate a 12-month rolling average
df['RA'] = df['Temp'].rolling(window=12).mean()
print(df.head())
```

Example Explanation:
- Adds a column with the 12-month rolling average of Temp.

5. Detect Anomalies

What is Detect Anomalies?
Identifies deviations from the mean for anomaly detection.
Syntax:
```
df['Anomaly'] = df['Temp'] - df['Temp'].mean()
```

Syntax Explanation:

- `df['Temp'].mean()`: Calculates the mean temperature.
- Subtracts the mean from each value to compute anomalies.
- Adds a column `Anomaly` with the deviations.

Example:

```
# Detect anomalies in temperature data
df['Anomaly'] = df['Temp'] - df['Temp'].mean()
print(df.head())
```

Example Explanation:

- Computes anomalies by subtracting the mean temperature from each value.

Real-Life Project:

Project Name: Monthly Temperature Trend Analysis

Project Goal:

Analyze monthly temperature trends over a decade, identify anomalies, and visualize patterns.

Code for This Project:

```
import pandas as pd
import matplotlib.pyplot as plt

# Load and prepare data
data = {
    'Date': pd.date_range(start='2010-01-01',
periods=120, freq='M'),
    'Temp': [20 + (i % 12 - 6)**2 * 0.5 for i in
range(120)]
}
df = pd.DataFrame(data)
df['Date'] = pd.to_datetime(df['Date'])
df.set_index('Date', inplace=True)
```

```
# Calculate rolling average and anomalies
df['RA'] = df['Temp'].rolling(window=12).mean()
df['Anomaly'] = df['Temp'] - df['Temp'].mean()
# Plot temperature trends
df[['Temp', 'RA']].plot(title='Monthly Temperature
Trends')
plt.show()
# Plot anomalies
df['Anomaly'].plot(title='Temperature Anomalies')
plt.axhline(0, color='red', linestyle='--')
plt.show()
```

Expanded Features:

- Combines rolling averages and anomaly detection.
- Visualizes trends and deviations effectively.
- Demonstrates integration of data preparation and analysis.

Expected Output:

- A line chart showing temperature trends with rolling averages.

- A chart highlighting temperature anomalies with a zero-reference line.

www.ingramcontent.com/pod-product-compliance
Lightning Source LLC
LaVergne TN
LVHW051435050326
832903LV00030BD/3099